Sacrifice in Pagan and Christian Antiquity

Sacrifice in Pagan and Christian Antiquity

Robert J. Daly

t&tclark
LONDON • NEW YORK • OXFORD • NEW DELHI • SYDNEY

T&T CLARK
Bloomsbury Publishing Plc
50 Bedford Square, London, WC1B 3DP, UK
1385 Broadway, New York, NY 10018, USA
29 Earlsfort Terrace, Dublin 2, Ireland

BLOOMSBURY, T&T CLARK and the T&T Clark logo are trademarks
of Bloomsbury Publishing Plc

First published in Great Britain 2019
This paperback edition published in 2021

Copyright © Robert J. Daly, 2019

Robert J. Daly has asserted his right under the Copyright, Designs and Patents Act,
1988, to be identified as the Author of this work.

Cover design: Tjaša Krivec
Cover images: (above) The Holy Trinity, engraving / after Pier Francesco Mola /
The Elisha Whittelsey Collection, The Elisha Whittelsey Fund, 1951 / THE MET;
(below) Four classical figures (pagan sacrifice), etching / Wenceslaus Hollar /
Purchase, Joseph Pulitzer Bequest, 1917 / THE MET

All rights reserved. No part of this publication may be reproduced or transmitted
in any form or by any means, electronic or mechanical, including photocopying,
recording, or any information storage or retrieval system, without prior permission
in writing from the publishers.

Bloomsbury Publishing Plc does not have any control over, or responsibility for, any
third-party websites referred to or in this book. All internet addresses given in this
book were correct at the time of going to press. The author and publisher regret any
inconvenience caused if addresses have changed or sites have ceased to exist, but
can accept no responsibility for any such changes.

A catalogue record for this book is available from the British Library.

Library of Congress Cataloging-in-Publication Data

Names: Daly, Robert J., 1933- author.
Title: Sacrifice in pagan and Christian antiquity / Robert J. Daly, S.J., Boston College.
Description: 1 [edition]. | New York: T&T Clark, 2019. |
Includes bibliographical references and index.
Identifiers: LCCN 2019016126 | ISBN 9780567687050 (hardback) |
ISBN 9780567687029 (epub)
Subjects: LCSH: Sacrifice–History. | Sacrifice–Christianity–History.
Classification: LCC BL570.D35 2019 | DDC 203/.409–dc23
LC record available at https://lccn.loc.gov/2019016126

ISBN: HB: 978-0-5676-8705-0
PB: 978-0-5677-0039-1
ePDF: 978-0-5676-8704-3
ePUB: 978-0-5676-8702-9

Typeset by Deanta Global Publishing Services, Chennai, India

To find out more about our authors and books visit www.bloomsbury.com
and sign up for our newsletters.

Contents

Foreword	viii
Part One Introduction, Methodological and Hermeneutical Issues	1
Preliminary notes	1
1 The history of religions	3
2 Postmodern approaches	5
3 The elites in Antiquity and Christianity	7
4 What is sacrifice?	8
5 The sacrificial world confronting ancient Christianity	11
6 Sacrifice in human history	13
7 The unity of the ancient world of sacrifice	17
8 The "end" of paganism?	19
Part Two The Greco-Roman Trajectory	21
1 From Homer and Hesiod up to Heraclitus and Plato	21
2 Anaximenes	27
3 Theophrastus	29
4 Philo of Alexandria	32
5 Apollonius of Tyana	33
6 Heliodorus of Emesa	34
7 Plutarch	35
8 Lucian	36
9 Porphyry	38
10 Iamblichus	39
11 Sallust	46
12 Symmachus	49
13 Macrobius and the "end" of paganism	51

Part Three	The Jewish-Christian Trajectory	53

Preliminary note: The many meanings of sacrifice ... 53
    1   General secular understanding of sacrifice ... 54
    2   General religious understanding of sacrifice ... 54
    3   Sacrifice in the Hebrew Scriptures ... 54
    4   General Christian understanding of sacrifice ... 55
    5   Specifically Catholic understanding of sacrifice ... 56
    6   Authentic Christian, that is trinitarian understanding of sacrifice ... 57

Transitional note ... 58

1 The Hebrew Scriptures ... 58
    a. The burnt offering ... 59
    b. Divine acceptance of sacrifice ... 60

Excursus 1: "Leave your gift there before the altar" (Mt. 5:24) ... 62
    c. Sin offering and atonement ... 63
    d. The blood rite and substitution ... 65
    e. From the Old Testament to the New Testament ... 67
    f. Qumran and the Dead Sea Scrolls ... 68

Excursus 2: Spiritualization ... 70

2 The Christian Scriptures (New Testament) ... 70
    a. Lack of liturgical-historical data ... 71
    b. Acts of the Apostles ... 72
    c. The gospels ... 73
    d. Paul and the Epistles ... 74
        1 The sacrifice of Christ ... 75
        2 Christians as the New Temple ... 75
        3 Sacrifice of/by Christians ... 76
        4 1Pet. 2:4–10 ... 77
        5 New Testament sacrifice is ethical ... 78
        6 The Epistle to the Hebrews ... 79

3 Early Christianity ... 79
    Preliminary note: The general situation ... 79
    a. *The Didache* ... 80
    b. Clement of Rome ... 81
    c. Ignatius of Antioch ... 82

d.	Justin Martyr and Athenagoras	82
e.	Irenaeus of Lyons	83
f.	Hippolytus of Rome	85
g.	Passover treatises	86
h.	Martyrdom and sacrifice	86
i.	Philo and the Christian Alexandrian tradition	87
j.	Barnabas	89
k.	Clement of Alexandria	89
l.	Minucius Felix	92
m.	Tertullian	93
n.	Cyprian	94
o.	Origen of Alexandria	95
p.	From Origen to Augustine	96
	aa. From Lactantius to Ephrem the Syrian	97
q.	Augustine	100
r.	Origen and Augustine compared	100
s.	The cult of the martyrs and the Eucharist	102
t.	The anaphoras of the fifth century	107

Excursus 3: A trinitarian view of sacrifice — 110
Excursus 4: The Eucharist as sacrifice — 114

Part Four   Select Points of Comparison and Contrast — 121

1. Prayer and sacrifice — 121
2. Divination and sacrifice — 123
3. Ethics, morality, and sacrifice — 125
4. The purpose of sacrifice — 127
5. The rhetoric of sacrifice — 129
6. The "economics" of sacrifice — 130
7. Heroes and saints — 132

Part Five   Concluding Summary and Looking Ahead — 135

Index of Names — 141
Subject Index — 145

Foreword

This modest-sized book has actually been more than a half-century in the making. Beginning in 1965 with research for a dissertation on *Christian Sacrifice* (published 1978) and culminating, so to speak, more recently with *Sacrifice Unveiled* (2009) and the long article in German on sacrifice for the *Reallexikon für Antike und Christentum* (*RAC*) (2014), it both takes up the main theme of my research career and, more importantly, opens up a window into some of the hermeneutical transformations that have been taking place as modern religious scholars attempt to read, instead of merely read into, religious antiquity.[1] What we present here is a revised and, with a view to making it more reader-friendly, greatly expanded version of the German article.[2]

Part of my initial motivation for attempting to write on sacrifice for the *RAC* was based on the naïve impression that it would afford an easy opportunity for a theologian to include in such a renowned reference work—it is an outstanding model of the historical criticism undergirding the classical history-of-religions approach—the specifically Christian, trinitarian understanding of sacrifice that I have been able to articulate in recent years, and that I can document is actually present, though often only implicitly, in some of the writings of Christian Antiquity. After three years of intensive work, that opportunity did indeed become reality with the 2014 publication of "Opfer" (see n. 1). But that task, and the subsequent task of transforming that article into a happily readable book in English, has been anything but easy. For, until then, I had paid little explicit attention to anything at all in non-Christian Antiquity, let

---

[1] Robert J. Daly, S.J., *Christian Sacrifice: The Judaeo-Christian Background before Origen*. Studies in Christian Antiquity 18 (Washington, DC: The Catholic University of America, 1978); summarized more accessibly in: *The Origins of the Christian Doctrine of Sacrifice* (Philadelphia, PA: Fortress Press, 1978); idem, *Sacrifice Unveiled: The True Meaning of Christian Sacrifice* (London/New York: T & T Clark/Continuum, 2009); idem, "Opfer," *Reallexikon für Antike und Christentum* (Stuttgart: Anton Hiersemann, 2014) 24.143–206.

[2] Some sections of the original "Opfer" article (corresponding to the following sections in this book: 3.1.f., pp. 68–69; 3.3.m.–n., pp. 93–95; and 3.3.p.aa., pp. 97–100) have been translated, modified, and adapted from what was originally written by Theresa Dockter (née Nesselrath), the talented German translator of this *RAC* article.

alone to the topic of sacrifice. I found myself, quite naively at first, delving into new and vastly complicated areas of research, areas that were themselves also undergoing profound hermeneutical transitions. For I was discovering that the so-called classical research methods that had been guiding critical research into the history of religions no longer reigned unchallenged. What I was undertaking involved bringing together several quite different methodologies and hermeneutical approaches—those of the history of religions and historical criticism, on the one hand, and those of traditional Christian history and theology, on the other. Further complicating this venture has been the fact that both of these methodological and hermeneutical approaches have themselves been undergoing transition. A helpful illustration of the complexity into which I was at first so naively diving can be found in some of the opening words of Alan Cameron's magisterial *The Last Pagans of Rome*:

> It is widely believed that pagans remained a majority in the aristocracy till at least the 380s, and then continued to remain a powerful force well into the fifth century (Ch. 5). On this basis the main focus of much modern scholarship has been on the supposedly stubborn resistance to Christianity. Rather surprisingly, they [the pagans] have been transformed from the arrogant philistine land-grabbers most of them were into fearless champions of senatorial privilege, literature lovers, and aficionados of classical (especially Greek) culture as well as the traditional cults. The dismantling of this romantic myth is one of the main goals of this book.[3]

Thus, this task, in which I have been generously aided by many old and new colleagues, has, because of the shifting ground on which this kind of research stands, turned out to be the most complicated one I have ever undertaken. But the experience of bringing it to some kind of fruition, or, put more modestly, the attempt to report for posterity on where this venture now stands, has become truly exciting. In the following pages I hope to communicate some of this excitement.

The excitement is due not just to the inherent nature of the topic, and what has been happening to it, but also to the several theological discoveries—"conversions" one might also call them—I have personally experienced in studying sacrifice over the past five decades. My early work, published in 1978,

---

[3] Alan Cameron, *The Last Pagans of Rome* (Oxford: Oxford University Press, 2011) 3.

based on my dissertation research in Mainz and Würzburg from 1965 to 1971 witnesses to the bubbling excitement of a young scholar enraptured by the discovery that he really could come up with something important on which others could build. Then, in the course of the 1980s, I discovered that it was not just systematic theologians but also, and often primarily, liturgical scholars who would be my major dialogue and research partners on the topic of "sacrifice." That gave my subsequent work a much more liturgical, worship-oriented, and at times even pastoral perspective than had previously been the case. Shortly after that, in the late 1980s, I also came in contact with and became an active member of the Colloquium on Violence and Religion (COV&R), an international, ecumenical, and interdisciplinary group of scholars and professionals dedicated to exploring the implications of René Girard's mimetic theory. For a detailed account of the theological significance of this, see pages 202–22 of my *Sacrifice Unveiled* (see above, n. 1).

The next major discovery or conversion took place in the late 1990s in the course of my editing for posthumous publication Edward Kilmartin's magisterial *The Eucharist in the West* (see p. 3, n. 4). It was in the course of that year-long task that I discovered the trinitarian reality of all true Christian sacrifice. It is that trinitarian reality and, indeed, that reality alone, that makes sacrifice truly and uniquely Christian, in contrast to its more general religious or secular meanings. That insight has become the focus of all my subsequent work on sacrifice, culminating in the abovementioned *Sacrifice Unveiled* (see above, n. 1). That was the immediate background from which I launched my research for the 2014 *RAC* article "Opfer" on which the this book is based.

But the discoveries/conversions haven't ended there! Most recently, in the course of "massaging" that *RAC* material into what I hope will be this happily more readable English book, I became aware of the particular way in which the perspective from which I had been, over the decades, happily deconstructing previous theories and accounts of sacrifice was itself in need of some deconstructing. For it was largely from the perspective of the great third-century Christian theologian Origen of Alexandria that I had been reading and deconstructing previous understandings and practices of sacrifice in Jewish and Christian Antiquity. For, back in the late 1960s, two years of intensive reading in and research on sacrifice in Origen immediately preceded and actually gave perspective to the research that resulted not just in *Christian Sacrifice* but, until recently, most of my subsequent work on this theme. Of course, Origen's unquestionable genius and massive influence on later Christian theology makes him, arguably, an ideal source for such a perspective; but the power of that perspective did, I now realize, leave me susceptible to some "reading into" the Christian data. My recent reading of Ullucci (see p. 2, n. 3) is what has brought me to this awareness. This recent new awareness, along with the extraordinarily wide-ranging collection of essays in *The Actuality of Sacrifice* (see p. 6, n. 11), makes me now more acutely aware that there is no—and perhaps never will be any—definitive and universally accepted definition of sacrifice. But what will remain, I hope to communicate, will be the excitement of learning more and more about it.

Part One

Introduction, Methodological and Hermeneutical Issues

Preliminary notes

First, there is no word in ancient Greek or Latin that corresponds precisely to what contemporary scholars think of as sacrifice. This is not merely because of the great variety of rites and ceremonies that modern scholars can call sacrifice or find associated with sacrifice in antiquity and across the breadth of the ancient Near Eastern, Mediterranean, and Western worlds. It is also because, according to a growing consensus of recent scholarship, the basic ideas of sacrifice that modern scholars have been finding in their study of Antiquity are dependent to a large extent on relatively modern concepts that we project back into the ancient world.

Second, however one defines it, a study of sacrifice in Antiquity and Christianity, while focusing on sacrifice in the first five centuries of the Christian era, must also be particularly attentive to its background and development in both early Greek and Roman Antiquity and in the entire ancient Hebrew religious tradition, as well as generally attentive to what was going on in the rest of the world in that "axial age."[1]

Third, the term "sacrifice" broadly understood includes or refers to the overwhelmingly massive variety of rites and actions by which people across the cultures and across human history have attempted to approach or somehow make contact with the world beyond, the world of the divine. For example, the five-volume *Thesaurus Cultus et Rituum Antiquorum*[2]

---

[1] "Axial age" is a term coined by Karl Jaspers (1883–1969) to refer to a "pivotal age" in several cultures in ancient history from about the eighth to the third centuries BCE.
[2] *Thesaurus Cultus et Rituum Antiquorum* (*ThesCRA*), 5 vols. (Los Angeles: J. Paul Getty Museum, 2004–05).

contains 5,352 columns of detailed information about the cultic practices of the ancient Mediterranean and Near Eastern world, most of it related in some way or other to "sacrifice." Further, when one asks an internet search engine about "sacrifice, early Christian," one is confronted with almost half a million "hits." A relatively brief book such as this, while aware of and making occasional use of that voluminously detailed background, must necessarily paint with broad brush strokes. Such brush strokes, because of the inevitable bias that enables and accompanies them, will inevitably ignore or obscure some details of what later research may well identify as significant detail.

Finally, it is with a specific Christian bias that I paint this picture. History is a story told by survivors and winners. For over a millennium and a half, Christians—and, basically, just the (culturally) Christian literate elite, and among them usually just the monks and theologians—have been practically the only ones painting this picture. That is now changing. In my own case, as already noted, it is only recently, in the course of studying Ullucci's work and attending more carefully to the recent authoritative work of Peter Brown and Alan Cameron,[3] that I have become aware of the *particular* inner-Christian bias in my own work. For, as already noted above in my Foreword, it was only after and obviously influenced by two years of intensive research into the idea of sacrifice in the early-third-century Christian theologian Origen of Alexandria that I began research into what became my foundational magnum opus, *Christian Sacrifice* (see above, p. viii, n. 1). It was from that Origenian perspective that I read—and inevitably read into—the biblical and Early Christian data; it was from that perspective that I attempted to deconstruct the way traditional scholarship looked at sacrifice in Antiquity and through the ages; and it is with a growing awareness of the strong bias in that perspective that I now undertake the task of also beginning to deconstruct some of my own previous research. Thus, much of what I do here will be an inevitably imperfect attempt to deconstruct some of these biases, including my

---

[3] Daniel C. Ullucci, *The Christian Rejection of Animal Sacrifice* (Oxford: Oxford University Press, 2012); Peter Brown, *Power and Persuasion in Late Antiquity* (Madison, WI: University of Wisconsin Press, 1992); idem, *Authority and the Sacred: Aspects of the Christianisation of the Roman World* (Cambridge: Cambridge University Press, 1995); idem, *The Rise of Western Christendom: Triumph and Diversity*, A.D. *200–1000* (The Agtrium, Southern Gate, Chichester, West Sussex: Wiley-Blackwell, 2013); Cameron, *The Last Pagans of Rome* (see above, p. ix, n. 3).

own. I leave it to my readers and to future scholars to continue this work—work that by its very nature can never be completely finished—toward that goal of full objectivity that is now increasingly recognized as one of modernity's fragile myths.

1 The history of religions

Heavily influenced by the great success of nineteenth- and twentieth-century history-of-religions research, most modern scholarship has tended to assume that bloody animal sacrifice is sacrifice par excellence. That kind of sacrifice became the conceptually unifying model or matrix for studying sacrifice both in general and in particular, and for investigating the great variety of religious rites and actions by which people in the ancient world attempted to express themselves in cultic-religious ways or, as it is often put by modern scholars, to approach or make contact with the world of the divine. However, the assumption that bloody animal sacrifice is the prime analogate of sacrifice is now increasingly criticized as projecting into this discussion, in an almost absolutizing way, a specifically Christian (some say Roman Catholic, others say Protestant, depending on who is being chosen to bear the blame) idea of sacrifice. This is because the nineteenth-century founding "fathers" of the history-of-religions school of thought were culturally—whether or not still actually persons of faith—Roman Catholic or Protestant intellectuals. As such, they were at least conceptually familiar in a positive (Catholic) or negative (Protestant) way with traditional Catholic teaching about the "unbloody" Sacrifice of the Mass being a "true" sacrifice.[4] Regardless of their acceptance or rejection of the Roman Catholic understanding of the Eucharist as a sacrifice, both camps characterized Christ's bloody crucifixion as a redemptive sacrifice, the founding moment of the Christian faith, the sacrificial act par excellence, that put an end to the validity or legitimacy of all further actual material sacrifice. This helps to explain why "Hubert and Mauss . . . the grandfathers

---

[4] As solemnly defined in the 1562 CE decree (DS 1751) of the Council of Trent. For full treatment, see David N. Power, *The Sacrifice We Offer: The Tridentine Dogma and Its Reinterpretation* (New York: Crossroad, 1989) and Edward J. Kilmartin, S.J., *The Eucharist in the West: History and Theology* (Collegeville, MN: Liturgical Press, 1998) 169–78.

of sacrificial studies within religious studies,[5] characterized sacrifice as fundamentally destructive."[6] It also helps explain why René Girard's early attitude toward sacrifice was so negative.[7]

Ironically, Hubert and Mauss, despite being quite "scientific" in their approach, were compounding basically the same methodological (and ultimately unscientific) error commonly made by the Protestant and Catholic reformers of the late sixteenth century. From that time, following the 1562 definition of the Council of Trent (see p. 3, n. 4), Catholics vigorously insisted that the Mass is a true and proper sacrifice (*verum et proprium sacrificium*). Protestants, however, were revulsed by their perception that the Catholics were turning the Sacrifice of the Mass into a human "work." Focusing sharply on the broadly shared Christian conviction that Christ's crucifixion was the perfect, once-for-all, and therefore unrepeatable sacrifice, Protestants had just as fiercely been denying that the Mass, that all Christians viewed in various ways as a "memorial" of the crucifixion, is a sacrifice. Both sides, in an ironically erroneous instance of (unconscious) ecumenical agreement—the irony[8] was truly tragic—tried to settle the question "scientifically." That is, in those early and relatively unsophisticated years of what became modern science and scholarship, they looked inductively at the way sacrifice was viewed and practiced in the various religions of the world. Finding that the destruction of a victim is common to and characteristic of sacrifice in those religions, both Catholics and Protestants agreed in making that destructive element the defining characteristic of what the Council of Trent was calling a "true and proper" sacrifice (see p. 3, n. 4). In common Christian teaching ever since the patristic age, Christians saw Christ as both the priest and victim in this unique sacrifice, and since all Christians believed that Christ is now risen in glory, he is obviously beyond all possible suffering or "destruction."

---

[5] Henri Hubert and Marcel Mauss, *Essai sur la nature et la fonction du sacrifice* (1898) ET: *Sacrifice: Its Nature and Function* (Chicago: University of Chicago, 1964).
[6] Katherine McClymond, *Beyond Sacred Violence: A Comparative Study of Sacrifice* (Baltimore: Johns Hopkins University, 2008) 150.
[7] René Girard, *La Violence et le Sacré* (Paris: Grasset, 1972) ET: *Violence and the Sacred* (Baltimore, MD: Johns Hopkins University/London: Athlone, 1977).
[8] For example, the renowned Methodist liturgical theologian Hoyt L. Hickman, upon hearing me expound a modern Roman Catholic understanding of eucharistic sacrifice, was heard to exclaim: "Gosh, if we had only known that four hundred years ago, we could have saved ourselves a lot of trouble!"

Thus, with Catholics resolutely insisting not only that the sacrifice of Christ is really present in the Mass, but also that the Mass is itself a "true and proper" sacrifice, an impartial judge would conclude that the Protestants easily won most of the debating points. And even in their intramural arguments, the Catholic theologians often found themselves standing on their heads in their efforts to explain their particular take on this central Christian mystery.[9] While sixteenth-century Christians, in the heat of their confessionally loyal polemics, may be excused for projecting their particular confessional Christian beliefs back into their understanding of what everyone was referring to as the sacrifice of Christ, the claims to scientific objectivity of the history-of-religionists three centuries later leave them much more open to criticism. In order to come up with their theories on the nature of sacrifice, Hubert and Mauss, and the many who followed them, had to overlook a great deal more of what was, by then increasingly, and by now overwhelmingly, the available evidence.

A further irony in this extraordinary story is that recent Roman Catholic liturgical scholarship, especially one main stream of it, has been pointing out that this Christian-influenced history-of-religions idea of sacrifice that so emphasized the destruction of a bloody victim as the central characteristic of authentic sacrifice is itself, as I have already suggested, an aberration, a misunderstanding, of the true nature of authentically Christian sacrifice.[10]

2 Postmodern approaches

Our contemporary postmodern world is not only increasingly suspicious of anything that sounds like a "great story," but also increasingly aware of the indigestible wealth of data from the ancient world: anthropological, historical, ethnological, cultural, epigraphical, archaeological, textual, etc., to which we

---

[9] See Robert J. Daly, S.J., "Robert Bellarmine and Post-Tridentine Eucharistic Theology," *Theological Studies* 61 (2000) 239–60.
[10] See Daly, *Sacrifice Unveiled* (see above, p. viii, n. 1). The main revisionist thesis of that book, favorably reviewed by both Protestants and Catholics, is in the process of becoming a consensual commonplace among theologians and liturgical scholars. See, for example, Mark S. Heim, *Saved from Sacrifice: A Theology of the Cross* (Grand Rapids, MI: Eerdmans, 2006). The pioneering nineteenth-century scholars of the history of religions, whatever their actual beliefs or nonbeliefs, were all—along with even their more traditionalizing religious opponents—embedded in, or at least deeply affected by, the Western Christian intellectual tradition.

now have access.¹¹ There no longer exists what one might call a "politically correct" and widely accepted methodological approach for painting a broad-brushed picture of sacrifice in Antiquity and Christianity. Recent scholarship, critically aware of the inadequacy of the traditional history-of-religions paradigms governing most modern readings of sacrifice in antiquity, is not yet in agreement about more adequate paradigms. This is richly illustrated by the undigested newness of some recent works on sacrifice.¹²

Petropoulou, from within a fairly traditional history-of-religions perspective, challenges the assumption that bloody animal sacrifice is the so-called prime analogate for understanding sacrifice in Antiquity. McClymond lends support to this challenge when she points out that vegetal rather than animal sacrifice was the primary sacrificial experience of most people in both the Vedic and the ancient Jewish cultures. She suggests that the Hubert-and-Mauss approach is possible only at the cost of ignoring a massive amount of other data. Heyman convincingly argues that focusing on "discourse" about sacrifice is key to understanding why it was the Christians and not the pagans who ultimately emerged victorious in what traditional scholarship has called the "battle over sacrifice." It is important to note here Ullucci's strong criticism of Heyman's presupposing the "critique model" of sacrifice. That model assumes that Christians rejected in principle all material sacrifice instead of, as Ullucci claims, just particular interpretations of sacrifice. Stroumsa, for his part, has convincingly argued that Christianity's Jewish origins and background, although neglected by many scholars, are key factors in understanding the "end of sacrifice." For, whether we use Stroumsa's *mutations* (French) or his

---

[11] See, for example, the five-volume *ThesCRA* (see p. 1, n. 2); see also the great variety of approaches in Alberdina Houtman, Marcel Poorthuis, Joshua Schwartz, and Yossi Turner, eds., *The Actuality of Sacrifice: Past and Present*. Jewish and Christian Perspectives 28 (Leiden/Boston: Brill, 2014).

[12] See, for example, Maria-Zoe Petropoulou, *Animal Sacrifice in Ancient Greek Religion, Judaism, and Christianity, 100 BC–AD 200* (Oxford: Oxford University Press, 2008); George Heyman, *The Power of Sacrifice: Roman and Christian Discourses in Conflict* (Washington, DC: Catholic University of America Press, 2007); Guy G. Stroumsa, *La Fin du sacrifice: Les mutations religieuses de l'Antiquité tardive* (Paris: Odile Jacob, 2005) ET: *The End of Sacrifice: Religious Transformations in Late Antiquity* (Chicago: University of Chicago, 2009; McClymond, *Beyond Sacred Violence* (see p. 4, n. 6 in Part 1); the recent collection *What the Gods Demand: Blood Sacrifice in Mediterranean Antiquity*, ed. Jennifer Wright Knust and Zsuzsanna Várhelyi (Oxford: Oxford University Press, 2012); and most recently, the still undigested challenge of works such as Daniel C. Ullucci, *The Christian Rejection* (see p. 2, n. 3); F. S. Naiden, *Smoke Signals for the Gods: Ancient Greek Sacrifice from the Archaic through Roman Periods* (Oxford: Oxford University Press, 2013); C. A. Faraone and F. S. Naiden, eds., *Greek and Roman Animal Sacrifice: Ancient Victims, Modern Observers* (Cambridge: Cambridge University Press, 2012); Houtman et al., *The Actuality of Sacrifice* (see above, n. 11).

English translator's *transformations*, it is a fact that within the space of a few hundred years (with most of the external changes taking place between 312 and 392 CE) bloody animal sacrifice passed from being apparently a central public religious activity to being juridically outlawed by the now-Christian emperors and thus, increasingly removed from the common experience of the general populace across the empire.[13] The most recent studies (see the final items above, in n. 12) have generally supported this picture of scholarship in transition and not yet in comfortable possession of a commonly shared hermeneutic for "reading" sacrifice in the ancient and modern world.

3 The elites in Antiquity and Christianity

The final paragraph of my "Preliminary notes" (above, pp. 1–3) mentions the "Christian literate elite." This refers to that very small part of the ancient Christian population who could read and write. From this tiny part of the Christian populace, possibly no more than 2 percent of the general Christian population, itself a very small part of the general population, came the bishops and others who recorded for posterity how they saw and understood their world. A similarly small percentage formed the non-Christian literate elite, often simply called "pagan"[14] by later Christian scholars. Intellectually, and to some extent culturally as well, these two groups, the Christian and the non-Christian literate elites, probably had more in common with each other than with their own popular masses. For example, the idea of different levels or kinds of "divine" beings or *daemons* that the Neoplatonists Porphyry and then especially Iamblichus used in order to ground their teaching on the appropriateness of different kinds and levels of sacrifices, some of that kind

---

[13] However, as Cameron reports (*The Last Pagans of Rome* [see above, p. ix, n. 3] 784–89), it was apparently well into the sixth century before pagan sacrifice faded from the imaginations of rigorist Christian preachers like Caesarius of Arles (470–542 CE).

[14] "There is some concern among biblical and religion scholars that the word 'pagan' is pejorative and unfairly judgmental"—Nijay K. Gupta, "'They are not Gods!' Jewish and Christian Idol Polemic and Greco-Roman Use of Cult Statues," *Catholic Biblical Quarterly* 76 (2014) 704–19, at 704 n. 1. For further discussion of this, see Gupta's reference to Hans-Josef Klauck, *Magic and Paganism in Early Christianity: The World of the Acts of the Apostles* (Edinburgh: T & T Clark, 2000) 1. Cameron devotes the entire opening chapter, "Pagans and Polytheists" (14–32) of *The Last Pagans of Rome* to justifying his use of the term "pagan" as a general designation for non-Christians in Antiquity.

of thinking betrays possible influence from the Christian writer Origen of Alexandria.¹⁵ One further and, in the context of this book, perhaps more obvious example of this is the actual content of the Christian polemic against pagan sacrifices. The Christians did not have to invent for themselves the idea that the gods (or the Divinity) have no need of sacrifice, or that it makes no sense to offer material sacrificial gifts to spiritual beings, or that the foibles and antics of the Olympian deities are myths not worthy of true divinity, let alone of human imitation. For the Christians, all this and more lay ready to hand in the writings of the philosophers, poets, and satirists—the pagan literate elite—in the non-Christian world around them. In dealing with their respective pagan or Christian adversaries these literate elites shared the same basic tactic favored by the enlightened positions of the literate elites in the other camp; indeed they often found much to admire in those positions. A favorite tactic, indeed one common to polemicists of all ages, was to pass over quickly—if indeed even to mention—what they shared in common, but rather, from their own elite and relatively unassailable high ground, to attack, often with notable schadenfreude, the vulnerably unenlightened ideas and practices of the nonliterate masses on the other side. But at least occasionally, as one sees in the pagan satirist Lucian (see Part 2.8., pp. 36–8) and in some of the Church Fathers, they were also critical of the unenlightened masses on their own side. And, one must also keep in mind that, in Antiquity, Neoplatonism provided the intellectual toolbox common to most of the elites, including the Christian elites. Indeed, all the elite of that epoch, whether Christian or pagan, shared in the same classical culture. As Cameron emphatically exclaims, "It was the only culture there was."¹⁶

4 What is sacrifice?

In using the word "sacrifice" we need to have in mind more than the general comments we have already made. But those comments do reflect a fairly strong assumption that there is not, and perhaps even cannot possibly be,

---

[15] See Heidi Marx-Wolf, "High Priests of the Highest God: Third-Century Platonists as Ritual Experts," *Journal of Early Christian Studies* 18 (2010) 481–513.
[16] Cameron, *The Last Pagans of Rome* (see p. ix, n. 3) 398.

a concise and adequate definition that could be used as a universally reliable starting point. Traditional scholarly approaches have often tried to identify a primary or basic idea of sacrifice from which to start. But such approaches no longer satisfy. The traditional view that, however one defines it, the central idea of sacrifice is to be found in or associated with bloody animal sacrifice is, as I have already pointed out, no longer accepted without question. However, since our work obviously needs more than just a few negative comments about what sacrifice is not, let me describe—or at least list—some of the things that this word "sacrifice" in the context of Antiquity and Christianity might mean or suggest. All the while we must keep in mind that, although we can identify a number of significant common elements in what the ancient non-Christian world was doing when involved in what modern scholars call sacrifice, Christians, for their part, insisted that they were not doing any of that. Christians, at least after the first few generations and after the definitive break with Judaism, insisted that sacrifice is not what Christians do. Sacrifice was what the Jews used to do in their Jerusalem Temple, and what pagans continued to do in and on their ubiquitous temples and altars. Increasingly, however, Christians, in the self-definition being articulated by their literate elites, were de facto using the rhetoric and language of sacrifice—whether we call it metaphoricized or spiritualized—to talk about their own religious lives and practices. This means, Ullucci convincingly argues, that Christians were not rejecting sacrifice as such, but only particular interpretations of it (see above, p. 2).

In other words, although Christians did not offer sacrifice, and were perceived by their contemporaries as not offering sacrifice, and although the heroically committed Christians made a point of strenuously resisting, even at the cost of their lives, any participation in sacrificial acts, no matter how routine or pro forma, they were in fact living profoundly sacrificial lives which their literate elites increasingly described in metaphorical, spiritualized sacrificial language. Further complicating this situation, but also confirming that this is what was actually taking place, is that the recently analyzed (mainly archaeological) evidence adduced by Ramsay MacMullen,[17] even if, as

---

[17] Ramsay MacMullen, *The Second Church: Popular Christianity A.D. 200–400* (Leiden/Boston: Brill, 2009).

claimed by his critics, somewhat overinterpreted by him, suggests that the vast majority of early, pre-Constantinian Christians did not regularly participate in the "official" worship of the Church. This was something that only 5 percent (MacMullen's perhaps overly low estimate) of early Christians regularly did. Rather, as a kind of "second church," the overwhelming majority of Christians (the other 95 percent) participated in the popular cult of the martyrs that took place in cemeteries and tombs. This was a popular religiosity that, both psychologically and externally, may have had a great deal in common with non-Christian popular religious practice. In any case, judging from some of their critical comments, it was something over which the Christian bishops did not have as much control as they would have wished.

This issue of control became increasingly important to the Christian bishops as, under the Christian emperors, their positions in society became not only more secure, but even dominant. Eventually, summing up the anti-pagan polemic of Caesarius of Arles (470–542 CE), Cameron writes, "Any ritual activity that was not unmistakably Christian, above all, any such activity that evaded his control, was pagan. . . . What most disturbed not just Caesarius but all the other bishops about New Year's customs was less their character, content, or purpose than the fact that rituals that gave such obvious and universal enjoyment were not only not Christian but beyond the control of the church."[18]

But, to come back to the earlier centuries, one needs, as we will see later (3.3.c., p. 82 and 3.3.s., pp. 102–7), only to read the words attributed to the martyrs Ignatius (died ca. 107 CE) and Polycarp (died ca. 155 CE) to see the extent to which Christians were appropriating the imagery, language, and rhetoric of sacrifice in a psychologically powerful way. For Christians, sacrifice was not, as it seems to have been for many non-Christians, a matter of offering some material object, however valuable, to some distant and perhaps disinterested god whose attention and favor needed to be gained, or even "bought." Rather, Christians were conscious of—at least potentially, if indeed called to martyrdom—offering not just some thing, but their very own bodily selves, in union/communion with the holy martyrs who had gone before them, and whose paths they knew themselves as possibly called to follow, and in union/communion with their God, Jesus Christ, who, anything but

---

[18] Cameron, *The Last Pagans of Rome* (see n. 3 in Foreword) 787–88.

disinterested, had already become human like themselves and given himself up sacrificially for them. In the cult of the martyrs they personally "communed" and identified with their heroes and models, with the divine Jesus Christ, and with the brothers and sisters who had gone before them in the very way that they themselves might be called upon to follow.

To be a Christian meant to accept the possibility of being called to suffer in the same way, and to see that possible event, however dreaded and painful, as it usually was, as the ultimate possible perfection of their human Christian lives. Thus, as Heyman[19] and Johnson,[20] among others, have pointed out, Christians had a story to tell about themselves, a deeply powerful story with which no pagan story could possibly compete. In terms of the "power of sacrifice," in terms of the "discourse about sacrifice," it really was an uneven battle. In terms of their "story," Christians occupied an unassailable high ground. Unless our Christian bias is totally misleading us in our reading of history, paganism had nothing like this with which to compete with Christianity. The great empire-wide persecutions of Decius (ca. 250 CE) and Diocletian (ca. 300 CE and following) can thus be seen as desperate rearguard actions in which the Christians, although politically still a powerless minority, actually, as the events of the fourth century eventually showed when the emperors had become Christian, already held the advantage in what proved to be effective rhetorical weapons.

5 The sacrificial world confronting ancient Christianity

What was it then that the Christians were, on the one hand, rejecting, and on the other hand, using as a source of the language and imagery with which they described their understanding of their own metaphorically spiritualized sacrificial lives? To answer this it helps, as McClymond put it, to see sacrifice as a polythetic event and to

> re-imagine sacrifice as a dynamic matrix of activity that does not privilege any single activity such as eating, killing, or exchange. Rather, we must

---

[19] Heyman, *The Power of Sacrifice* (see p. 6, n. 12).
[20] Maxwell E. Johnson, "Martyrs and the Mass: The Interpolation of the Narrative of Institution into the Anaphora," *Worship* 87 (2013) 2–22.

attend to the obvious fact that a number of different activities regularly occur during sacrificial events, activities that can be arranged into several general types like: selection, association, identification, killing, heating, apportionment, and consumption.[21]

(1) *Selection*, for example, refers to the activities involved in identifying, procuring, and preparing the appropriate sacrificial substance, whether animal or non-animal. It is a precondition for any of the other activities that constitute a sacrifice. (2) *Association* refers to activities that publicly link an oblation with one or more deities. This would seem, at first glance, to be more important in polytheistic than in monotheistic traditions, but even in monotheistic Israelite sacrifices, there were rituals that highlighted the obvious association with YHWH in contradistinction to the god(s) of their surrounding communities. (3) *Identification*, the human correlate of association, "refers to the practice of correlating an offering with a ritual patron" (McClymond 30), that is, those by whom or for whom the offering is being made. (4) *Killing* refers to "the intentional execution of the offering."[22] However, it is not, as she rightfully insists, synonymous with destruction or violence. It also never stands alone but is always connected with other actions which may have more ritual significance than the act of killing itself. With a critical eye toward some traditional Christian theorizing, she insists, "The surprising presence or absence of killing language in certain sacrificial contexts has important implications for sacrificial theorizing, especially when that theorizing depends upon images of death, substitution, and bloodshed."[23] (5) *Heating* refers primarily to placing an offering on top of a sacrificial fire, but it is also a broad concept that can also include a number of activities like cooking, or the action of purifying oblations in order to prepare them for subsequent ritual manipulation. (6) *Apportionment* is a key procedure that highlights the constructive rather than destructive aspects of sacrificial activity. It refers to the division of a material offering into multiple pieces or portions, and the assigning of these portions for distribution to the various ritual recipients or participants. (7) *Consumption* includes, but is not limited

---

[21] McClymond, *Beyond Sacred Violence* (see p. 4, n. 6 in Part 1) 29.
[22] Ibid., 30.
[23] Ibid., 31.

to, eating. It refers to "the ingestion of the sacrificial offering either by the ritual participants—priest or laity (or both)—or by the god(s) involved in being recipients of the sacrifice."[24] It is both remarkable and significant how similar these seven activities are to different aspects of the Hebrew biblical sin offering (3.1.c. pp. 63–65).

Sometimes all seven of these activities, or activities like these, are performed, and sometimes only a few. No one of them, just by itself, would be a sacrifice. McClymond suggests that the number and extent of them, along with the complexity of their interrelationships, can provide a general, external rule of thumb for estimating just how "sacrificial" a given ceremony or event might be. Such an outline of the components of an event that can be referred to as a sacrifice, even if it turns out to be only provisional, or eventually superseded by something better, has the merit of providing us with a helpful working description/definition of sacrifice in Antiquity. This is what the Christians were, on the one hand, rejecting and, on the other hand, so Ullucci (see p. 2, n. 3 and p. 14, n. 26), interpreting and appropriating as a source of the language and imagery for their own reinterpretation of sacrifice and self-definition as Christians. It gives us a description or definition that will enable us to begin the comparing and contrasting that is implied in the "and" when one speaks of "Sacrifice in Pagan and Christian Antiquity."

6 Sacrifice in human history[25]

Before taking up sacrifice in its Greco-Roman and Jewish-Christian trajectories, it will help to look briefly at the location of sacrifice in the overall trajectory of human history. The farther we go back, the more do we find ideas about sacrifice clouded in the mists of prehistory and myth. Scholars do not agree even about the approximate time when sacrifice began to be practiced by human beings. Some scholars link sacrifice to a specific stage of developing human sociality, namely those relatively advanced post-hunter-gatherer cultures in which durable goods began to be passed on through fictive or real

---

[24] Ibid., 32–33.
[25] We sketch here with a very broad brush a relatively small trajectory within the vast areas of history and scholarship that are alluded to in, for example, the twenty-five essays gathered in Jeffrey Carter, ed., *Understanding Religious Sacrifice: A Reader* (London/New York: Continuum, 2003).

extended kinship groups. In the Western world this corresponds to the period roughly from 8000 BCE to 500 CE.[26] Others, like René Girard, link sacrifice to the (presumably) much earlier origins of religion and human culture.[27] A fascinating aspect of this discussion is the indisputable fact that, whatever the merits of this or that historical reconstruction of the origin of sacrifice, all can agree on 500 CE as the approximate end date for its public flourishing in the Western world, a date that also coincides with the approximate end date for our study of "Sacrifice in Pagan and Christian Antiquity." For our purposes in this book, it is expedient to begin with the millennium before the Christian era. Then, as our "story"[28] develops, we will be focusing on its two main poles of experience and reflection: First, Greco-Roman sacrifice, the practice of and attitudes toward sacrifice in the ancient Mediterranean world broadly understood, and second, the sacrificial ideas and practices, and, eventually, theological theorizing, of the Judaeo-Christian tradition.[29]

From about the millennium before the Christian era, the time from which we begin to have written historical records produced by the various literate elites, there seems to have been in the ancient Near Eastern and Mediterranean world, at least in general, a significant common and *practical*[30] understanding about what sacrifice was. In the Jewish traditions about the Exodus, for example, it was clear that Moses did not have to explain what sacrifice was when he tried to get Pharaoh to let the Jewish people go out into the desert to offer sacrifice (Exodus 3–12). And, reading between the lines, it seems clear that Pharaoh knew that if he let them do that, he would be in danger of losing them, not just because they would then be beyond the reach of his horses and chariots, but also because they would be beyond the pale of Egyptian religion

---

[26] See Daniel C. Ullucci, "Before Animal Sacrifice: A Myth of Innocence," *Religion and Theology* 15 (2008) 357–74.

[27] See further details and discussion about the debate on this in Jonathan Z. Smith, "The Domestication of Sacrifice," in Robert G. Hammerton-Kelly, ed., *Violent Origins: Walter Burkert, René Girard, and Jonathan Z Smith on Ritual Killing and Cultural Formation* (Stanford, CA: Stanford University Press, 1987) 191–235.

[28] "Story" refers to our attempt to explain sacrifice in Antiquity. The scare quotes are to remind us that the "history" of sacrifice, whether Christian or pagan, does not, as recent scholarship emphasizes, have one logical, continuous, diachronic line of development on which scholars commonly agree.

[29] Our sources will perforce be mainly literary. The practice of bringing data that is nonliterary—that is, material, sociological, ethnographical, etc.—to bear on (especially) ancient history is a scholarly art still in its infancy.

[30] We emphasize *practical* understanding. There was in Antiquity, especially before Christians began "reinterpreting" it, little theorizing, let alone agreement, about the meaning of what moderns refer to as sacrifice.

and thus also the control of Egyptian authority. Similarly, too, no one in the Homeric epics needed to be told what sacrifice was, and why sacrifice was important in their attempt to win the attention/favor/support of the gods for themselves and their particular wishes and needs.

Thus, taking roughly 1000 BCE as our first point of entry into the history of ideas about sacrifice, we do not find great external differences between the sacrificial practices of the Jewish people and their neighbors across the Near Eastern and Mediterranean world. Despite the great differences in details that modern scholarship can so carefully document, people pretty much knew and took for granted what sacrifice was and what it did or claimed to do. And—painting now with a very broad brush—this was basically still the case at the beginning of the Christian era. The inhabitants of Antiquity, Christian as well as non-Christian, were, in the words of Heyman, "steeped in a sacrificial world" (xv) in which, for example, "the Romans used their sacrificial discourse to maintain political power and create Roman identity . . . convinced—[as Symmachus still was in the late fourth century (see 2.12., pp. 49–50)] that without proper exercise of these religious rites, the fragile balance of the cosmos and the empire would cease to exist."[31]

But by this time, however, some basic ideas about sacrifice and its role in the human and cosmic world were definitely changing. For example, developments that, in Judaism, had already led to an idea of spiritual sacrifice, and that in Christianity had already led to the appropriation of the language of sacrifice while fiercely rejecting its actual practice, such developments had already taken place. Much of this had to do, of course, with changing/developing images of the divine in Greek religious philosophy, beginning at least as far back as Plato, and perhaps even Hesiod, as well as in Judaism itself. Late biblical Judaism had been developing its incipiently spiritualized appropriation of the language of sacrifice for and to a God who has no need of it, more or less at the same time that the religious thinkers and philosophers of the Greek world had been figuring out approximately the same thing. It may not be irrelevant to note that, in this so-called axial period, Buddhism, Hinduism, Jainism, Zoroastrianism, and Confucianism in the East had been making similar "moves." But while the Greco-Roman world came to this understanding primarily via reason, the

---

[31] Heyman, *The Power of Sacrifice* (see above, p. 6, n. 12) xvii.

Jewish-Christian world came to it primarily via revelation. Whether, when, and to what extent "Athens" and "Jerusalem" were mutually influencing each other might well be argued,[32] but they were unquestionably experiencing somewhat parallel developments.

The route via "reason" came about through the developing realization that the gods (or "the god," or the divine in general in the more sophisticated thinking of the philosophers) are immaterial, are spiritual, and thus cannot be touched or affected by material offerings. But this achievement of the philosophers, that is, of that aspect of the "literate elite" of the ancient world, seemed to have had little effect on the widespread public and private religious practice by which people continued to offer sacrifice in the traditional, material way. All the while, however, this philosophical achievement was introducing a theoretical weakness into serious thinking about traditional sacrificial practices that must have played a part in, or at least helped to pave the way for, the eventual disappearance of broadly practiced public material sacrifice that was already well under way by the end of the fourth century CE. For those who for philosophical-religious reasons were critiquing sacrifice were also, generally (for practical-political reasons?) recommending or at least allowing it in actual practice.[33] This was an inconsistency that other critiquing positions, such as those taken by the Christians, did not hesitate to exploit.

The route via "revelation" is basically the "story" that over the years I have been telling in several books and articles.[34] It is the story of the gradual spiritualization of sacrifice in the Jewish-Christian tradition that (1) began with the awareness, documented early in the Hebrew Scriptures, that sacrifice is useless if it is not accepted by God, and (2) continued with the deepening awareness that this divine acceptance, as the prophets emphasized, will not be granted in the absence of the proper ethical dispositions in those offering the sacrifice. Then (3) in Late Biblical Judaism, stimulated by the experience of Exile and Diaspora in which material sacrifice could not be offered (by that time the Torah allowed valid sacrifice to be offered only in the Jerusalem Temple) these ethical dispositions and other religious or good works began

---

[32] The argument, in these terms, seems to go back to Tertullian's (ca. 155–ca. 240 CE) challenging question in *De praescriptione haereticorum*: "What has Athens to do with Jerusalem?"

[33] On this point, see the comment by Ullucci quoted toward the end of the section titled: "The unity of the ancient world of sacrifice" (see p. 18).

[34] See, among others, the works listed on p. 17, n. 36.

even to take the place of and substitute for material sacrifice. In other words, in this line of thinking, it was not the fact of the material offering itself that made the sacrifice effective, but rather the fact that it was offered *in accordance with the Law*. Carrying out the works of the Law (prayer, study of the Torah, works of justice and peace, carrying out the spiritual and corporal works of mercy, etc.) is what made sacrifice effective/acceptable to God and eventually (in practice for the Jews who still longed for the return to the Jerusalem Temple, and in principle for the Christians) totally took the place of material sacrifice. This is the position that the Christians made their own when, but certainly not at first,[35] they rejected material sacrifice as a useless "work" of the Law (as practiced by the Jews) or, even worse, as an idolatrous work (as practiced by the pagans). All the while however, the Christians, and apparently not just the Christian elite, were, in their reinterpretation of sacrifice, appropriating the language and rhetoric of sacrifice, as we can see with Ignatius and Polycarp, in order to describe their personal identification with and communion with the sacrifice of Christ and the sacrifice of the martyrs.[36]

7 The unity of the ancient world of sacrifice

Although modern scholarship has been pointing out (1) that little or nothing in the ancient world corresponds precisely to what is now called "sacrifice," and (2) that the practices in the ancient world that can be described as "sacrificial" are staggering in their number, variety, and pluriformity; it is nevertheless still possible—as well as, for our purposes in this book, necessary—to talk in general terms about sacrifice in the ancient world. That is because, among other reasons, Roman religion, the dominant religion in the world of Christian Antiquity, "originated from within a matrix of Greek influence."[37]

---

[35] See the section: "Early Christian Positions on Sacrifice," in Ullucci, *The Christian Rejection* (see p. 2, n. 3) 69–118.
[36] For further details, see Daly, *Christian Sacrifice* (see p. viii, n. 1); idem, *The Origins of the Christian Doctrine of Sacrifice* (ibid.); idem, *Sacrifice Unveiled* (ibid.); "New Developments in the Theology of Sacrifice," *Liturgical Ministry* 18 (Spring 2009) 49–58; idem, "The Trinitarian Christ-Event: A Different Sacrifice," in *The Ambivalence of Sacrifice*, Luiz Carlos Susin, Diego Irrazaval, and Daniel Pilario, eds. = *Concilium* 2013/4 (London: SCM, 2013) 100–8.
[37] Heyman, *The Power of Sacrifice* (see above, p. 6, n. 12 in Part 1) 11.

While, therefore, as ritual practice, "sacrifice [then as now] refuses any simple description or definition ... it continues to be appropriated by human cultures to constitute meaningful identity.... To be Roman was to be religious. To be religious was to sacrifice in a variety of specified and ritually controlled ways."[38] Thus, to refuse, as faithful Christians did, to offer sacrifice was perceived by serious-thinking pagans, for example, Celsus (ca. 170 CE), as being a perverse threat to Roman order, power, and balance. Remember, the Roman mind, in common with most thinking in Antiquity, did not distinguish between the religious and the profane. Thus, the Roman authorities saw the Christians, who did participate in at least some aspects of public Roman life, and claimed to be good citizens, being arbitrary in refusing, in their rejection of sacrifice, to participate in some of its critically important aspects. The pagan Celsus was right in perceiving this as a serious threat, as the events of the fourth century eventually showed. And even when Origen, seven decades after Celsus, undertook (in about 245 CE) to provide a Christian answer to him,[39] it was anything but clear that it was the Christians who would end up victorious in this struggle.

Regarding this "struggle," Ullucci convincingly argues that it was not just a struggle between pagans and Christians as such, but between "cultural producers," struggling not for or against sacrifice as such, but to define their own idea of proper or ideal sacrifice. He writes,

> The vast majority of authors whom scholars have labeled critics of sacrifice actually support the practice wholeheartedly. This group includes the Platonic, Stoic, Epicurean, and Skeptic philosophers; Greek dramatists; Greek and Roman Satirists such as Menander and Lucian; Hebrew Bible authors such as the authors of I Samuel, Psalms, Hosea, Isaiah, and Jeremiah; other Judean writers such as Philo; and many more.[40]

Eventually, so Ullucci, the struggle came down to which Christian group would, in course of the fourth century, become victorious, that is, over Arianism,

---

[38] Ibid., 43.
[39] Notably, Origen did not challenge Celsus's accusation that Christians, in refusing to serve in the military, were shirking their civic duties; Origen argued rather that their duty was to fight for the empire and the emperor with spiritual but not material weapons. That was a time when it could still be argued that the more the world became Christian, the less would material weapons be needed (Origen, *Against Celsus* 8.73). See John Helgeland, Robert J. Daly, and J. Patout Burns, *Christians and the Military: The Early Experience* (Philadelphia, PA: Fortress Press, 1985) 39–44.
[40] Ullucci, *The Christian Rejection* (see above, p. 2, n. 3) 6.

over various gnosticisms, and over whatever else the eventual "victors" would label as heterodox. They did this by synchronically and harmonizingly synthesizing a number of disparate positions into a—however amorphously defined—single orthodoxy. This eventually became the process of reinscribing "a modern (largely Christian) narrative upon the history of animal sacrifice" (Ullucci 5, [see p. 2, n. 3]). Contemporary scholarship makes this massive paradigm-changing challenge possible, but has not yet had the time to "digest" it into a commonly accepted consensus position.

8 The "end" of paganism?

Numerically, by about the year 375 CE, more than half a century after the conversion of Constantine, the Christians, however secure and, under the Christian emperors, however influential they had become, were still a minority in the Roman Empire. Nominally, at least, most of the population was still pagan. But after another fifty years, at the approximate time of the appearance of Macrobius's *Saturnalia*, most of the population had become at least nominally Christian. What one could call Roman culture was ready to move into the beginning stages of becoming a Christian culture. Cameron helps us to make broad-brushed sense of this by identifying five different but overlapping categories of people. On one side were the "committed Christians" (like Ambrose and Augustine), but balanced on the other side by the "committed pagans" (like Praetextatus and Symmachus), with the "committed" including the occasional "rigorist." Then, further, on the Christian side would be the "center-Christians"; these would include "both time servers and sincere believers who were nevertheless not interested in or well-informed about details of theology and saw no reason to reject secular culture." Balancing these would be the "center-pagans"; they would include "people brought up as pagans but with no deep investment in the cults themselves." And "in between" these Christian and pagan groups "would be the (for a time) perhaps rather large group of those who for one reason or another resisted straightforward classification." Cameron sums up the situation as follows:

> I would not suppose that there was ever more than a relatively small proportion of the entire population in either of the "committed" groups.

The major shift, as I see it, would be from the center-pagan to the center-Christian category. From about 340 to (say) 430 I would guess that some three-quarters of the one passed into the other.[41]

Once that change was taking place, the end of paganism, the end of a dominant culture in which material and animal sacrifice could have a recognized place, was but a matter of time.

---

[41] Cameron, *The Last Pagans of Rome* (see p. ix, n. 3) 176–77.

Part Two

The Greco-Roman Trajectory

1 From Homer and Hesiod up to Heraclitus and Plato

The Homeric epics, more or less from the middle of the eighth century BCE, recount a significant variety of sacrificial practices, but offer little or no reflection on their meaning, either for those participating in them or for the culture which took them for granted. Whatever ideas of sacrifice or theories of sacrifice that have been found in or can be gleaned from the two great Homeric epics, the *Iliad* and the *Odyssey*, are, more often than not, retrojections of relatively modern ideas back into that time. In contrast, Hesiod's[1] two works, *Theogony* and *Works and Days* from a century or so later, constitute our sole source that tells us anything at all, in its own terms and not just in what we read into them, about what is thought about sacrifice at that time. There is a brief passage that seems to refer to sacrifice to, or sacrifice with a prayer to, the goddess Hecate:[2]

> She ... [Hecate] ... is honored most of all by the immortal gods. For even now, whenever any human on the earth seeks propitiation by performing fine sacrifices according to custom (*kata nomon hilaskētai*), he invokes Hecate; and much honor very easily stays with that man whose prayers the goddess accepts with gladness, and she bestows happiness on him, for this power she certainly has. For of all those who came forth from Earth and Sky and received honor, among all these she has her due share. (*Theogony* 414–22)[3]

Despite the brevity of this passage, the modern reader can note (1) that "sacrificing fine offerings *kata nomon*—according to custom" assumes that

---

[1] Hesiod was a post-Homeric Greek epic poet from about 700 BCE.
[2] In Greek mythology Hecate was a goddess of Thracian origin identified with Artemis and the moon, and also with Persepone, the goddess of the infernal regions, and accordingly regarded as presiding over magic and witchcraft—(*The New Shorter Oxford English Dictionary*, s.v.).
[3] Our translations of Hesiod are from Glenn W. Most, *Hesiod I: Theogony, Works and Days, Testimonia*, LCL 57 (Cambridge, MA/London: Harvard University Press, 2006).

the hearers of the poem know both what sacrifices are and what "according to custom" means. One can also note (2) the presence of the common and practically universal connection of sacrifice with petitionary prayer. It is also clear (3) that the granting of the prayer is not automatic; it seems to be at the discretion of the god even if the offering and the prayer (the connection between them is implicit) is faithfully carried out "according to custom." And finally, (4) the words "she has her due share" allude to the pervasive issue of the division/distribution of power, benefits, blessings, and sacrificial shares both among the gods and their human beneficiaries.[4]

But far more famous is the mythic passage, later in the *Theogony*, containing Hesiod's particular take on the Promethean story of the origin of sacrifice:

> For when gods and mortal men were reaching a settlement in Mecone, with eager spirit he [Prometheus] divided up a great ox and, trying to deceive Zeus' mind, set it before him. For he set down on the skin before him the meat and the innards, rich with fat, hiding them in the ox's stomach; and then he set down before him in turn the ox's white bones, arranging them with deceptive craft, hiding them with gleaming fat. Then the father of men and of gods addressed him: "Son of Iapetus, eminent among all rulers, my fine fellow, how unfairly you have divided up the portions!" So spoke in mockery Zeus, who knows eternal counsels; but crooked-counseled Prometheus addressed him in turn, smiling slightly, and he did not forget his deceptive craft: "Zeus, most renowned, greatest of the eternally living gods, choose from these whichever your spirit in your breast bids you." So he spoke, plotting deception. But Zeus, who knows eternal counsels, recognized the deception and did not fail to perceive it; and he saw in his spirit evils for mortal human beings—ones that were going to be fulfilled too. With both hands he grasped the white fat, and he became enraged in his breast and wrath came upon his spirit when he saw the ox's white bones, the result of the deceptive craft. And ever since then the tribes of human beings upon the earth burn white bones upon smoking altars for the immortals. (*Theogony* 535–57)

Schlegel is not alone in pointing out that "the text is resolutely ambiguous about how fully Zeus was deceived."[5] Pötscher, however, goes well beyond this

---

[4] See in Part 1.5., p. 12, subsections (6) and (7) regarding the *apportionment* and *consumption* aspects of sacrifice.

[5] See *Theogony* and *Works and Days*, trans. and introd. Catherine M. Schlegel and Henry Weinfield (Ann Arbor: University of Michigan, 2006) 6.

and argues that Zeus is really in complete control.[6] But whatever the case—for the text of Hesiod that has been transmitted to us does not make everything fit neatly—Prometheus, the "crooked-schemer" trickster, seemingly gets the better of it, not only at this point, but then also when the narrative goes on to relate how he manages to steal fire from Zeus for human use. But eventually Zeus gets the upper hand and takes his revenge, beginning with—an early literary instance of explicit misogynism—his creating woman to be the bane of man's existence. To our modern eyes, as we now read as a written text what was originally an oral epic, the passage strongly emphasizes, although it does not explain why it is, (1) that sacrifice offered "according to custom—*kata nomon*" is integral to the "settlement," that is, the right relationship that is being arranged (*ekrinonto*) between the gods and human beings. The narrative also points out (2) how desperately important is the proper division of the sacrifice between the gods and humans (again the *apportionment* and *consumption* aspects). Clearly underlying the whole narrative is also what becomes pervasively important in later sacrificial practice, namely (3) the aspect of "calculation" involved in choosing and dividing up a sacrificial offering, and (4) the obvious implication that, in doing this, one cannot with impunity "play games" with the gods, as Prometheus did. Prayer (5) also has a role in offering sacrifice, as we can see in the dialogue between Zeus and Prometheus—although here, the "prayer" of Prometheus is more the mouthings of a larger-than-human trickster than the words of a human properly subservient to the gods. Finally, (6) implicit in this mythic account is the idea that the gods want, desire, and somehow even need the (eventually sacrificial) gifts of human beings.

Later in the *Theogony* there is a passage that, despite its ambiguity, makes very clear what seems already implicit in the previous ones, namely, that the gods themselves also have binding obligations within the etiologically still-being-articulated but, in the mind of the author, and presumably of the listeners too, already-taken-for-granted, system of things:

> A tenth portion has been assigned to her [Hecate]. For nine-fold around the earth and the broad back of the sea he [a lesser God in competition

---

[6] Walter Pötscher, "ΟΣΤΕΑ ΛΕΥΚΑ: Zur Formation und Struktur des olympischen Opfers," *Grazer Beiträge* 21 (1995) 29–46.

with Hecate] whirls in silver eddies and falls into the sea, and she as one portion flows forth from the crag, a great woe for the gods. For whoever of the immortals, who possess the peak of snowy Olympus, swears a false oath after having poured a libation from her, he lies breathless for one full year; and he does not go near to ambrosia and nectar for nourishment, but lies there without breath and without voice on a covered bed, and an evil stupor shrouds him. (*Theogony* 789–98)

In *Works and Days*, however, we find ourselves in a new key. This later didactic poem of Hesiod is not just mythic but also part of a long-established tradition of Mediterranean and Middle Eastern wisdom literature that has obvious analogues with some parts of the Hebrew Scriptures that are actually contemporaneous with it. No longer recounting a tale of mythic origins, Hesiod is now speaking, exhorting, teaching in his own voice to his fellow men. We are now being addressed with a significant ethical, and, yes, even social concern. This seems to be a clear early example of the working of a "literate elite" in contrast to the popular, traditional-mythical ideas about sacrifice that we find in the *Theogony*:

> Property is not to be snatched: god-given is better by far. For if someone grabs great wealth with his hands by violence, or plunders it by means of his tongue, as often happens when profit deceives the mind of human beings and Shamelessness drives Shame away, then the gods easily make him obscure, and they diminish that man's household, and wealth attends him for only a short time. It is the same if someone does evil to a suppliant or to a guest, or if he goes up to his own brother's bed, sleeping with his sister-in-law in secret, acting wrongly, or if in his folly he sins against orphaned children, or if he rebukes his aged father upon the evil threshold of old age, attacking him with grievous words; against such a man, Zeus himself is enraged, and in the end he imposes a grievous return for unjust works.
>
> But as for you, keep your foolish spirit entirely away from these things. According to your capability, make holy sacrifice to the immortal gods in a hallowed and pure manner, and burn splendid thigh-pieces on the altar; at other times, seek propitiation with libations and burnt-offerings, both when you go to bed and when the holy light returns, so that their heart and spirit will be propitious to you, so that you may barter for other people's allotment, not someone else for yours. (*Works and Days*, 320–41)

One summary of the content of these lines reads: "What they [the gods] give is much better than plunder, for they easily ruin the miscreant. Sacrifice and pray to them, and they will favour you."⁷ As we examine the written text more closely with our modern eyes, the following points stand out. *First*, it is notable that here, in a work apparently composed some years after the more mythic *Theogony*, Zeus, now no longer a mythic, anthropomorphic god in a violent struggle for supremacy, has become the much more serene, benign father of the gods, the supporter of righteous, and the punisher of unrighteous actions.

Second, in an age when it is a "prosperity gospel" that some popular Christian preachers insist on preaching, we moderns quickly notice how central a place in the value system is being given to property and material prosperity. This particular dense passage of only twenty-two lines begins and ends and never strays far from that theme. Forbidding the wrongful acquisition of property or wealth, whether it is done by force or by deceit, is the first-mentioned in Hesiod's "pentalogue" of negative commandments. In a seemingly subordinate position are the remaining four "commandments": not to wrong a suppliant or visitor; not to steal your brother's wife; not to wrong orphans; not to abuse your aged father. Line 335 then strongly exhorts Perses (the addressee of Hesiod's exhortation) to keep his heart/soul/mind (*thumos*) from such witless or dim-witted things (*aesiphrona*). In other words, what is bad about them is not so much that they are (in modern terms) immoral, what's bad about them is that they are ill-advised and irrational.

Third, without transition, Hesiod shifts to what would correspond to the first table of the Hebrew Decalogue: obligations to the divine. "According to your capability (*kad dunamin*) make holy sacrifice (*erdein hier*) to the immortal gods in a hallowed and pure manner, and burn splendid thigh pieces on the altar." Hesiod obviously assumes that his hearers recognize this reference to the central religious action of his culture, the usually quite public ceremonial sacrificing of a large animal. The phrase "according to your capability" is pregnant with meaning since only a wealthy person could ever have the means to offer such a sacrifice, and even such a person must do so only in moderation, that is, according to and not beyond his means. That this, even for a person of means, would not be an everyday affair is the obvious import of the "at other times (*allote*) to seek propitiation (*hilaskesthai*)" both night and morning with libations and burnt offerings (*spondēsi thuessi*) so that their

---

⁷ Martin L. West, *Hesiod: Works and Days* (Oxford: Clarendon Press, 1978) 2.

heart and mind (*kradiēn kai thumon*) may be propitious (*hilaon*) toward one becoming successful in gaining and holding property and possessions.

The phrase "according to your capability" is also an early instance of what becomes a commonplace when most philosophical and religious traditions, and not just Judaeo-Christianity, talk about the monetary value of a sacrifice. Commenting on this phrase West writes: "Xenophon says that Socrates used to quote this line with approval, arguing that a poor man's sacrifice should be just as pleasing to the gods as a rich man's" (*Mem.* 1.3.3).[8] In addition, the phrase "at other times—*allote de*" alludes to the fact, often overlooked by modern readers that, for obvious economic reasons, the experience of sacrifice for most of the people most of the time was not with the more spectacular large-animal blood sacrifices, but with the much more ordinary and everyday, usually vegetal, offerings.

Somewhat later, Heraclitus (ca. 540–480 BCE, one of the earliest in the Greek philosophical tradition) distinguished between two kinds of sacrifice: the kind offered by those relatively few people who are, interiorly, fully purified, while the other kind of sacrifice is material.[9] It is against the latter that Heraclitus polemicizes, calling the purification that is intended by the shedding or manipulation of sacrificial blood a defilement (*Besudelung*).[10] Developing basically the same point one hundred years later, and expressing a religious and ethical insight that, in general terms, had a strong appeal for all thinking persons, pagan as well as Christian, Plato taught that the gods accept homage/worship only from people who, like the gods themselves, are morally pure.[11] A few centuries later, Seneca, the Roman Stoic philosopher (4 BCE–65 CE) also taught exactly the same thing: that the gods are to be worshiped not "by sacrifices and streams of blood, . . . but by a clean heart and a worthy intention."[12] For Seneca, in common with most serious thinkers on the matter, taught that what decides the quality of the sacrifice is, above all, the rectitude of the sacrifice and not the size or lavishness of what is sacrificed. If that rectitude is lacking, the sacrifice, no matter how great, cannot do any

---

[8] Ibid., 240
[9] VS 22 B 69.
[10] VS 22 B 5; cf Arnold Angenendt, *Die Revolution des geistigen Opfers: Blut, Sündenbock, Eucharistie* (Freiburg: Herder, 2011) 27.
[11] Leg. 4, 717a; Angenendt, *Die Revolution des geistigen Opfers* 28.
[12] Frg. 123 (42 Haarse).

honor to the gods.¹³ And indeed, a few centuries after that, the perduring power of this general insight helps explain the strength of Donatism (the belief that the validity of the sacraments is completely dependent on the holiness of the minister) among North African Christians of the fourth and fifth centuries.

2 Anaximenes

Shortly after Plato (427–347 BCE) we come to the *Rhetoric to Alexander*. Although traditionally included in the works of Aristotle (384–322 BCE), it is now generally recognized as coming from the rhetorician/historian Anaximenes of Lampsacus (380–320 BCE). This treatise on the principles of political oratory, similar in structure (but without the examples) to Aristotle's *On Rhetoric*, first lists seven subjects about which public speeches can be given: (1) religious ritual, (2) legislation, (3) the form of the constitution, (4) alliances and treaties, (5) war, (6) peace, and (7) finance. Devoting hardly more than one full page[14] to religious ritual, the first of these subjects, Anaximenes states that one can speak about the rites of religion with a view (1) to maintaining the established ritual as it is, or (2) to altering it either to a more splendid form, or (3) to a more modest form.

Regarding the first of these three options, Anaximenes first notes that universal reverence for ancestral customs supports the performance of sacrifices in the ancestral manner. Arguing further from expediency, Anaximenes points out that following tradition in this way will be advantageous, either for individuals or for the community, on the grounds of economy, or of honor, or of pleasure, or of practicability. This assumes, he notes, that there has been neither deficiency nor extravagance in these celebrations (1423 a30–b9).[15]

Anaximenes also finds plausible arguments in favor of the second option, of altering the rites in the direction of greater splendor. Amplification, he notes, is

---

[13] *Benef.* 1, 6, 3; cf. 4, 9, 1. For the idea of thank-offering as being the only proper human response to divine beneficence, see Angenendt, *Die Revolution des geistigen Opfers* (see above, p. 26, n. 10) 29.

[14] Deceptively dense, this seems to be the earliest of the few Greek texts that even begins to talk about the meaning and purpose of sacrifice.

[15] Following the standard mode of referencing the works of Aristotle within which this particular work is contained.

not destruction, and "in all probability even the gods show more benevolence towards those who pay them more honour" (1423 b15f). And in any case, Anaximenes adds, this is not only how our forefathers actually acted, it is also, in general, in accordance with the way we normally administer our affairs.

But there are also reasons and conditions that can argue for the third option, a reduction to a more modest form. The most obvious of these reasons is when the populace is less prosperous and the state of finance is weaker. In that case both gods and men judge it to be great folly to do things beyond one's capacity and, what a modern reader finds most significant—and also in line with Plato's teaching noted above—"it is not the cost of the sacrifices but the piety of those who offer them that give pleasure to the gods" (1423 b28f).

Anaximenes then sums it all up in a few sentences that begin to sound like what a modern reader might call a definition of or theory of sacrifice:

> Let us now define what is the best form of sacrifice, in order that we may know how to frame proposals and pass laws for its regulation. The best of all sacrificial ceremonies is one organized in a manner that is pious towards the gods, moderate in expense, of military benefit, and brilliant as a spectacle. It will show piety to the gods if the ancestral ritual is preserved; it will be moderate in expense if not all the offerings carried in procession are used up; brilliant as a spectacle if lavish use is made of gold and things of that sort which are not used up in the celebration; of military advantage if cavalry and infantry in full array march in the procession. (1423 b34–1424 a5)

Despite its brevity (only 1423 a30–1424 a12) in Aristotle's works, this single paragraph is a remarkably rich guide to what, at least in the mind of its author, a ruler needs to know about sacrifices.

But one must keep in mind that this is not a philosophical treatise but a practical handbook for public speakers, written in the literary form of a letter addressed to Alexander the Great. It does not discuss sacrifice directly, but only how to speak about sacrifice. That religion/sacrifice is mentioned first suggests either its importance in the mind of the author, or perhaps only that, in a nod to traditional public opinion, it is something that needs to be gotten out of the way before going on to other matters, for, after its relatively brief treatment here, the subject does not come up again. The modern reader must also keep in mind that it is the public civic authority, and not some supposedly different or independent religious entity, that has the responsibility for organizing and overseeing things religious, and to do that specifically for the benefit and advantage of both individuals and the community. It is not the primary concern of this work, but only when Anaximenes comes to possible reasons for expanding or reducing the sacrifices that things more resonant with modern sensitivities come to the surface. For here he ventures into what is presumably going on in the mind of the gods. This begins to be theology. Assumed to be behind all this, of course, is the unchallenged traditional idea, however vaguely and variously understood it might be, that the gods somehow desire, want, or perhaps even "need" the sacrifices; that the gods may show more benevolence to those who pay them more honor; and (somehow in tension with this) that both gods and men judge it to be folly to sacrifice too much, since it is probably not the cost of the sacrifice but the piety of those offering it that most pleases the gods. This is, in substance at least, not very far from the later Christian idea of the widow's mite (Mk 12:41–44; Lk. 21:1–4) or the earlier insistence of the Jewish prophets that God prefers justice and mercy over sacrifice.

3 Theophrastus

Roughly contemporaneous with Anaximenes is the philosopher and scientist (often called the "father of botany") Theophrastus (ca. 371–ca. 287 BCE). Possibly a young student of Plato, he most certainly had a close association with Aristotle whom he succeeded in the leadership of the Peripatos when Aristotle left Athens after the death of Alexander in 323. His teaching on sacrifice is contained mostly in *On Piety*, a work we know only from its extensive quotation and expansion centuries later in the *De Abstinentia* of the Neoplatonist, Porphyry (ca. 232–303 CE). Scholars do not agree in separating out precisely where Theophrastus ends and Porphyry begins, so we will content ourselves with dealing with Theophrastus primarily as mediated to us by Porphyry. In addition to the foundational study of Bernays,[16] our main guide will be Dirk Obbink.[17]

---

[16] Jacob Bernays, *Theophrastos' Schrift über Frömmigkeit: ein Beitrag zur Religionsgeschichte, mit kritischen und erklärenden Bemerkungen zu Porphyrios' Schrift über Enthaltsamkeit* (Berlin: Wilhelm Hertz, 1866, repr. Hildesheim/New York, 1979).

[17] Dirk Obbink, "The Origin of Greek Sacrifice: Theophrastus on Religion and Cultural History," in William W. Fortenbaugh and Robert W. Sharples, eds., *Theophrastean Studies on Natural Science, Physics and Metaphysics, Ethics, Religion, and Rhetoric*; Studies in Classical Humanities 3 (New Brunswick [USA] and Oxford [UK]: Transaction Books, 1988) 272–95.

While Porphyry was using Theophrastus's objections to animal sacrifice to bolster his own theoretic defense of neo-Pythagorean vegetarianism, Theophrastus's own purpose seems to have been more simple and straightforward, namely, to find the most appropriate way to honor the gods. In a much-quoted passage he teaches,

> There are altogether three reasons why we sacrifice to the gods: to show them honor (*dia timēn*), to give them thanks (*dia charin*), or to express our need for some benefit (*dia chreian*). Just as though we were dealing with good men (*agathois andrasin*) so we consider that it is necessary to give first fruits to the gods. We honor the gods while trying to turn aside misfortune or obtain benefits for ourselves or when we have already been well treated by them or simply through appreciation of their favorable disposition toward us. (*De Abst.* 2.24.1)[18]

Examined philosophically, this brief passage expresses a basically functionalist attitude toward religion and religion's primary ritual expression in the practice of sacrifice. Its concept of piety, like that of Aristotle (1250 b22), "makes piety a component of justice, first toward the gods, then toward other humans, and so on."[19] This "and so on" suggests that Theophrastus sees issues of justice and injustice as applying not just between the gods and humans, but also between humans and the (specifically domestic) animals, which relationship should preclude humans from killing them. When this is examined theologically, and mindful how sacrifice and prayer are so closely connected (see 4.1., pp. 121–23), one is struck by how remarkably similar these "three reasons" are to Jewish and Christian ideas about the basic twofold structure of prayer as consisting of two "movements": First, anamnetic (praise and thanksgiving for the gifts of creation and redemption) and, second, epicletic (petition for one's desires and needs).[20]

Finally, like Hesiod before him and like so many others to come after, Theophrastus supports his basic ideas by reporting, or even inventing—and he does seem to have done both—etiologies of ritual. He reports basically the

---

[18] As cited by Obbink, "The Origin of Greek Sacrifice" (see above, p. 29, n. 17) 282–83.
[19] Ibid., 283; see *De Abst.* 2.22.1–25.7.
[20] For example, see Part 3.3.s. and t., pp. 102–10.

same cause/origin, as do other sources, for the prehistoric institution of the Attic *bouphonia*, "the 'ox-slaying' for Zeus of the city (*Dii Poliei*) which was performed on the fourteenth day of Skirophorion in midsummer, at the altar of Zeus on the highest spot of the Athenian acropolis."[21] But much more original with Theophrastus seems to be his extensive "invented tradition"[22] in which he accounts for the origin of sacrifice as a process that began in a first stage "at some incalculable time in the distant past . . . long before trees," when humans offered up only grass and such plants "to the gods of heaven" (*De Abst.* 2.5.1–2). Then, in a second stage, after the discovery and development of agriculture, humans offered the first fruits of the cultivated produce of the land (*De Abst.* 2.6.1–3). Animal sacrifice, however, begins only with a third phase when, at a time of famine, humans were reduced to cannibalism, which then morphed into human sacrifice, and then into substituting the bodies of animals in place of their own (*De Abst.* 2.27.1–6). Within this invented "cultural history"[23] that Theophrastus develops, one can discern an ambiguous combination of motives: optimistic, regarding the various developments of culture, but also pessimistic with regard to the ongoing religious "development," that in his mind was a degeneration. But it seems also to be precisely this ambiguity that enables Theophrastus to explain such contrasting things as atheism and religious excess. For some people revile the gods for taking honor from such a practice as animal sacrifice, while others go overboard in the opposite direction, trying to curry divine favor with "even more unjustly extravagant sacrifices."[24]

To sum up, Theophrastus clearly teaches that we should offer modest and reasonable sacrifices in order to honor the gods, and to give them thanks, and to petition them for our needs. Following the leads of Plato and Socrates, he teaches, though not as forcefully as did the Hebrew prophets, that it is also important that we do this with the proper dispositions of mind and soul. He does not, however, clearly develop precisely what he means by that.[25] Following

---

[21] Obbink, "The Origin of Greek Sacrifice" (see p. 29, n. 17) 284; see *De Abst.* 2.29.1–31.1.
[22] See Eric Hobsbawm's introduction to *The Invention of Tradition* (Cambridge: Cambridge University Press, 1983).
[23] Obbink, "The Origin of Greek Sacrifice" (see p. 29, n. 17) 279.
[24] Ibid., 280.
[25] See P. A. Meijer, "Philosophers, Intellectuals and Religion in Hellas," in Hendrik S. Versnel, ed., *Faith Hope and Worship: Aspects of Religious Mentality in the Ancient World* (Leiden: Brill, 1981) 216–62, at 245–59.

the somewhat revisionist argument of Obbink, it seems that Theophrastus felt that, on the grounds of natural kinship with animals, humans probably *should* feel aversion to blood sacrifice. And while he notes approvingly Empedocles's (490–430 BCE) rejection of it, he himself does not polemicize against it. Rather, he seems, regretfully, to take it for granted as part of human cultural development, or, as in this particular case, religious degeneration. Since he did not cite any actual instances of it, we can cautiously assume that he probably did not actually know of any historically verifiable instances of abstention from animal blood sacrifice.

4 Philo of Alexandria (see also below, 3.3.i., pp. 87–89)

The Jewish religious philosopher Philo (ca. 20 BCE–50 CE, roughly contemporaneous with St. Paul) represents a high point both in the cultic spiritualizing already well under way in the Jewish tradition, and also a high point in the allegorical interpretation increasingly practiced in the Greco-Roman literary and philosophical traditions. He is also foundational for the Christian appropriation, especially by the Alexandrians, of this spiritualizing and allegorizing. Much of this can be summed up in the following seven points:[26] (1) The Passover (Judaism's foundational religious feast that Philo saw not as a cultic ritual but as the life of virtue culminating in the mental turning toward education and wisdom) is a symbol of the soul's upward progress. (2) True sacrifice is thus an "offering" of the whole self: the soul, the mind, and the heart. (3) The divine acceptance of sacrifice, along with the primacy of the religious-ethical dispositions of the one making this "offering," is absolutely essential. (4) The purpose of sacrifice is primarily to honor God and only secondarily to benefit the worshiper. (5) His idea of the high priest, that in his mind is almost equated with the divine Logos, oscillates between Jewish idealization and Hellenistic spiritualization. (6) The idea of universal priesthood—an office or duty that is conferred primarily by ethical purity rather than cultic ritual—is central to his thinking on sacrifice. (7) His statements that had the most

---

[26] See Daly, *Christian Sacrifice* (see p. viii, n. 1) 389–422 and *The Origins of the Christian Doctrine of Sacrifice* (see ibid.) 104–10.

influence on Christian thinkers tended to center on the realities and symbols of temple, sanctuary, and altar. For example:

> There are, as is evident, two temples of God: one of them this universe, in which there is also as high priest his First-born, the divine Word, and the other, the rational soul, whose priest is the real man; the outward and visible image of whom is he who offers the prayers and sacrifices handed down from our fathers.[27]

> The true altar of God is the thankful soul of the Sage, compacted of perfect virtues unsevered and undivided, for no part of virtue is useless. On this soul-altar the sacred light is ever burning and carefully kept unextinguished, and the light of the mind is wisdom, just as the darkness of the soul is folly.[28]

For the appropriation and development of this by the Christian Alexandrians, see below, 3.3.*i.–k.* (pp. 87–92) and o. (pp. 95–96).

5 Apollonius of Tyana

Apollonius was a neo-Pythagorean philosopher who lived from ca. 15–ca. 100 CE. There are no directly surviving works. We know about him primarily from Philostratus the Elder (ca. 170–247 CE) who, almost two centuries later, wrote his novelistic and hagiographic *Life of Apollonius of Tyana*. This popular work described him, quite possibly as a pagan counter to the gospel accounts of the Christian Jesus, as a wandering ascetic philosopher and wonder-worker. In a fragment of his lost work on sacrifice, *peri thusiōn*, quoted in the late third century by the Neoplatonist philosopher, Porphyry,[29] and again, quoted perhaps more exactly, in the early fourth century by the Christian, Eusebius of Caesarea,[30] Apollonios, while (esp. according to Porphyry) distinguishing between the different levels of divine beings to

---

[27] *De somniis* 1.215; see also *De plantatione* 50; *Quis rerum divinarum heres sit* 75.
[28] *De specialibus legibus* 1.287.
[29] Porphyry, *De abstinentia* 2.34.
[30] Eusebius, *Praeparatio evangelica* (Sources Chrétiennes 256, p. 144); see Eduard Norden, *Agnostos Theos: Untersuchungen zur Formgeschichte religiöser Rede* (Stuttgart: B.G. Teubner, 1971) 39–41, 343–46.

whom sacrifice is due,[31] insists that absolutely nothing material is to be offered to the supreme God: "Hereafter it is not under any circumstances allowable to offer sacrifice to the great and supremely sublime God."[32] However a total rejection of sacrifice does not seem consonant with what little we know of the life of Apollonios. By the fourth century, widespread popular hagiographical embellishment had turned Apollonios into a saintly theurgic wonder-worker, a pagan rival to Jesus of Nazareth. He was appealed to by the Christian as well as by the pagan literate elites in their polemic against material sacrifice, especially bloody animal sacrifice.

6 Heliodorus of Emesa

Some time in the third Christian century,[33] quite possibly after, and influenced by, Philostratus's *Life of Apollonius* (see above, pp. 33–34), Heliodorus wrote his popular Greek historical novel *Aethiopica*, also known as *Ethiopic Tales*. This is a work that may come as a surprise to those who assume that the genre of a fantastical adventure story filled with violence, love, and sex is one of civilization's later "achievements." Sacrifices are taken for granted throughout this novel. And, fortunately for us, Book 3 contains a vivid description of an elaborate hecatomb sacrifice at Delphi that gives preciously unique witness to how the popular mind in the third century CE envisioned that a festive hecatomb[34] would be celebrated at a major pagan sanctuary at the turn of the millennium.[35] Described in luxurious detail is the procession of ornately decorated sacrificial animals, one hundred oxen plus similar numbers of other animals, along with their festally clad "conductors," and the flute players, and the singing and dancing maidens, plus squads of mounted cadets, plus their brilliantly clad leader whose indescribable male beauty was surpassed only by the womanly beauty of the priestess emerging from the temple of Artemis,

---

[31] This is similar to Iamblichus's conception of the different levels of divine beings (see below, pp. 39–46).
[32] Ibid.
[33] Or, possibly, in the second half of the fourth century, after the reign of Julian—see Robin Lane Fox, *Pagans and Christians* (New York: Alfred A. Knopf, 1987) 137.
[34] A hecatomb was an ancient Greek or Roman celebration in which one hundred cattle were sacrificed.
[35] For a general introduction to these *Ethiopic Tales*, see Gerald N. Sandy, *Heliodorus* (Boston, MA: Twayne, 1982).

she "the object of all men's prayers, he of all women's" (*aeth*. 3.4).[36] When all was ready, "the women ululated, the men shouted, and then, as at one signal, oxen, lambs, and goats were sacrificed (*hiereuonto*), as if the slaughter had been carried out by a single hand."[37] In its closing pages many chapters later, the novel reflects the state of popular opinion by celebrating, on the one hand, the end of human sacrifice[38] but not, despite the wishes of the presumably fictional Ethiopian gymnosophists[39]—who probably symbolized the hopeful dreams of the philosophers of Heliodorus's own day—the end of animal sacrifice (*aeth* 10.9).[40]

7 Plutarch

The voluminous writings of Plutarch, ca. 40–ca. 120 CE, a middle Platonist and, so Griffiths, a "philosophical monotheist"[41] who in his later years served as a priest of Apollo at Delphi, contain, as one might expect, numerous references to sacrifice. There is, however, typical of the extent to which sacrifice could be simply taken for granted in the ancient world, little description of the ritual of sacrifice and little discussion of its meaning and purpose. Parallels with Christian ideas and writings do abound, especially in the *Moralia*,[42] but there are no direct references to Christianity beyond his apparently implicit inclusion of it among the "superstitions." For example: "Nothing is more pleasing to the gods, whether sacrifice or ritual enactment, than the true belief about them, thus you will avoid superstition, which is no less evil than atheism."[43]

---

[36] Heliodorus, *Aethiopica* 3.4, as translated by Moses Hadas, *Heliodorus: An Ethiopian Romance* (Philadelphia, PA: University of Pennsylvania, 1999, repr. of University of Michigan, 1957) 71.
[37] Ibid., 3.5, p. 72.
[38] Ibid., 10.39, p. 276.
[39] In the ancient world there were several references (e.g., in Aristotle, Plutarch, Lucian, and Porphyry—see Liddell and Scott, *s.v.*) to the *gymnosophistai*, the naked philosophers of India. Their appearance here seems to serve little purpose beyond novelistic titillation.
[40] Ibid., 10.9, pp. 250–51.
[41] John Gwyn Griffiths, *Plutarch's de Iside et Osiride* (Cardiff: University of Wales, 1970) 19.
[42] See Hans Dieter Betz, *Plutarch's Theological Writings and Early Christian Literature* (Leiden: Brill, 1975) and *Plutarch's Ethical Writings and Early Christian Literature* (Leiden: Brill, 1978).
[43] Plutarch, *De Iside et Osiride* 11.355C.

8 Lucian

This brings us to the satirical cynic-philosopher-sophist Lucian of Samosata (ca. 115–ca. 200 CE). His *De Sacrificiis* is classified as a diatribe, a kind of informal chat or sermon on a moral theme. But the title, "On Sacrifices," is a misnomer—possibly an insertion from the scribal pen of a later Byzantine monk—since it deals not just with sacrifice but also with other aspects of religious ritual such as prayer to the gods and beliefs about them.[44] Although *De Sacr.* shows throughout signs of hasty composition, its opening words powerfully express what Lucian thinks about his subject:

> When considering the behaviour of poor fools (*hoi mataioi*) at their sacrifices, festivals and processions in honour of the gods, the objects of their prayers, their vows and their beliefs about the gods, I don't know if anyone is so doleful and grief-stricken that he won't laugh at the stupidity of what goes on, and I think a much more immediate reaction than laughing will be to wonder whether these men should be called pious (*eusebeis*) or on the contrary sacrilegious wretches (*theois echthrous kai kakodaimonas*) in thinking the gods (*to theion*) so abject and ignoble as to have any need of men to enjoy being flattered and to be angry when neglected. (*De Sacr.* 1)

Later, after his irreverently mocking "ascent to heaven" on, as he facetiously puts it, the "wings" of Homer and Hesiod, Lucian describes with unmistakable satirical—even sardonic—glee the absurd behavior of the Olympian pantheon:

> "And the gods, by the side of Zeus ensconced" (*Iliad* 4.1),—for majestic language is appropriate, I think, since I'm up above—fix their gaze on the earth and look round in every direction in the hope of seeing somewhere fire being lighted or the savour of sacrifice rising "a-twirling round the smoke" (*Iliad* 1.317). If anyone sacrifices, they all have a feast, open-mouthed, eager for the smoke, and drinking blood poured by the altars, behaving like flies. But if they eat at home, they have nectar and ambrosia for dinner. In olden times, moreover, men would feast and drink with them—I refer to Ixion and Tantalus—but because they behaved outrageously and talked too much, they are still being punished to this day, and heaven is out of bounds and forbidden to all mortals. (*De Sacr.* 9)

---

[44] See Matthew D. Macleod, *Lucian: A Selection* (Warminster, England: Aris & Phillips, 1991) 276.

Rarely has the soft underbelly of popular, traditional Greco-Roman religion been so fiercely and embarrassingly exposed. Lucian, of course, as customary with the literate elites and polemicists generally, is attacking a straw man; for he takes his examples of indefensible religious credulity not from his fellows among the pagan intellectual elite, nor from the contemporary cults flourishing all around him—although in his *On the Death of Peregrinus* he does allow himself a few by-the-way anti-Christian jabs—but from the old myths and stories about the Olympian gods.[45]

As is his custom, Lucian is having his fun at the expense of the foibles, superstitions, and pretensions and foolish beliefs of those around him. But lurking just beneath the surface, between the lines, and behind the biting humor, there is also something very serious going on. Yes, Lucian can indeed be serious, as is obvious from his *How to Write History*, "the only monograph on the theory of historiography to have survived from classical literature."[46] When, in that work, he turns from his outrageously witty examples of bad history, and tries to explain and give examples of good history, he betrays more than just a touch of seriousness. Although serious writing is not his métier, there is still quite a bit in Lucian from which even the modern historian can learn. The fools (*hoi mataioi*) who offer sacrifices he calls not pious (*eusebeis*) but sacrilegious wretches (*theois echthrous kai kakodaimonas*) literally "demon-possessed enemies of [the] gods" because they think so abjectly of the gods (literally "the divinity—*to theion*"). In other words, although there is no indication that Lucian is a religious believer, behind his criticism seems to be the relatively mature religious-philosophical idea of a non-anthropomorphic, nonmaterial divinity that, by his day, had become common among the Greco-Roman intelligentsia, the "literate elite" that he respected and with whom he identified, and for whose amusement and bemusement he wrote. His final words, with its *agnoia/anoia* Greek pun, sum it up:

> These practices [that de facto began to be outlawed by the Christian emperors just 200 years later] and general beliefs don't seem to me to need anyone to criticize them, but rather a Heraclitus or a Democritus, one to laugh at people's ignorance—*agnoia*, the other to lament their folly—*anoia*. (*De Sacr.* 15)

---

[45] Ibid., 10.
[46] Ibid., 283.

Such criticism, expressing trenchantly so much of the thinking and attitudes of the "literate elite" in the Roman Empire, is one of the reasons why Symmachus's attempts, two centuries later, to defend traditional Roman religious ritual, seem to be, if one looks back sympathetically on the plight of the pious pagans of Antiquity, such a sad, doomed-to-failure, and even tragically hopeless rearguard action (see 2.12., pp. 49–50).

9 Porphyry

Porphyry (ca. 233–ca. 303 CE), a student of Plotinus (ca. 204–270 CE) and a giant among the Neoplatonist philosophers, devoted almost half of book 2 of his *de abstinentia* (on abstinence from animal food) to quoting Theophrastus's (see 2.3., pp. 29–32) neo-Pythagorean aversion to, but not absolute rejection of, animal sacrifice (*De Abst.* 2.5–33). He immediately followed that with a paraphrase of Apollonius's insistence that absolutely nothing material should be offered to the highest God (*De Abst.* 2.34). However, his mention, in this paraphrase, of the different sacrifices that they are fit to offer to different powers, as well as what he writes later in *De Abst.* 2.44, indicates that his rejection of animal sacrifice, like that of Theophrastus, is also not absolute. Thus, one is left wondering whether it is only a Neoplatonist's "pure" aversion to theurgy[47] that might be behind the apparently radical rejection of material sacrifice in his *Letter to Anebo* that (his own gifted disciple?) Iamblichus (see 2.10., pp. 39–45) felt obliged to refute in *De Mysteriis*. In any case, Porphyry's *De Abstinentia* 2, and then Iamblichus's *De Mysteriis*, and Sallusti's later appropriation of Iamblichus, when taken together, come close to providing us with what would seem to a modern reader to be at least the beginning of a pagan, or at least non-Christian, theory, or even "theology," of sacrifice. But among these, because of the philosophical depth and sophistication and even the

---

[47] "Theurgy," in one of its meanings, refers to "a system of white magic originally practised by the Egyptian Neoplatonists, performed by the invocation and employment of beneficent spirits." That would more than suffice to explain Porphyry's visceral rejection. But so would the more general definitions of theurgy as "the operation or intervention of a divine or supernatural agency in human affairs; the results of such action in the phenomenal world," or "the art or technique of compelling or persuading a god or beneficent or supernatural power to do or refrain from doing something"—see *The New Shorter Oxford English Dictionary* (Oxford: Clarendon Press, 1993) and *Webster's Ninth New Collegiate Dictionary* (Springfield, MA: Merriam-Webster, 1990) s.v.

incipiently theological implications of his writing, Iamblichus, as we will now see, stands quite alone in the ancient world as paganism's crown witness for a serious theory of sacrifice.

10 Iamblichus

The Greek-writing Iamblichus (ca. 250–ca. 330 CE) was known as the chief Neoplatonist philosopher of the Syrian school. It is not clear whether or not he was once a disciple of Porphyry (ca. 232–ca. 303 CE), but it is clear that he eventually became Porphyry's critic, most especially in his *De Mysteriis* (ca. 280–305 CE), a work that he wrote, it would seem, to counter objections coming from the later Porphyry's anti-religious skepticism. Iamblichus strenuously objected (1) to the way that Porphyry, with and following Plotinus (the Neoplatonist philosopher and mystic, 205–270 CE), overvalued the ability of the human soul to achieve union with the divine, (2) to their consequent undervaluing of cultic ritual, and (3) to their general rejection of material and animal sacrifice. For Iamblichus, such sacrifice was essential to the—at least initially theurgic—process of humans achieving union with the divine.[48] As we will see in our subsequent treatment of Sallust (below 2.11., pp. 46–49), it was from Iamblichus and his school that Julian the Apostate (Emperor 361–363 CE) apparently learned the Neoplatonism that he used as a weapon against Christianity.[49]

References to sacrifice are scattered throughout the *De Mysteriis* (*DM*), but most of them are concentrated in Book 5 (*DM* 5.1–26 [199–240])[50] that is devoted to "the question of sacrifices" (*DM* 5.1 [199]). On the whole, *DM* contains the most extensive treatment of sacrifice to come from non-Christian Antiquity. It is, in effect, the only instance from that milieu—especially when taken in conjunction with and as a corrective to Porphyry—of what modern scholars would call a detailed theory of sacrifice.[51] In fact, a "theology

---

[48] See Scott Bradbury, "Julian's Pagan Revival and the Decline of Blood Sacrifice," *Phoenix* 49, no. 4 (Winter 1995) 331–56.
[49] See "Iamblichus," in *Oxford Dictionary of the Christian Church*, 3rd ed. (1997) 814.
[50] Our Iamblichus quotations and translations are from the edition of Emma C. Clarke, John M. Dillon, and Jackson P. Hershbell, *Iamblichus: De Mysteriis* (Atlanta, GA: Scholars Press, 2003).
[51] We are assuming that Sallust's work (see below 2.11., pp. 46–49) is a simplified derivative of Iamblichus.

of sacrifice" is what modern theologians would see being unfolded here; for what Iamblichus is doing here somewhat approximates the traditional Christian meaning of theology as "faith seeking understanding." The opening pages of this document (*DM* 1.1–2 [1–7]) carefully distinguish between the theological, the theurgical (how and why sacrifice actually "works"), and the philosophical. For example, Iamblichus, thinking basically as did the authors of the somewhat later Christian "Mystagogical Catecheses,"[52] points out that some things, apparently referring specifically to the theurgical, "require experience of actions" (*DM* 1.2 [6]). For there are, in other words, things that the uninitiated will not be able to understand. For a skeptic like Porphyry, no matter how brilliant, if he has not been initiated, the higher truths of theology may be beyond his capabilities.[53]

At first, *DM* seems to be Iamblichus's response to a seemingly random series of questions about sacrifices. But it is actually a detailed refutation of Porphyry's *Letter to Anebo*, a vicious attack on the kind of theurgy taught by Iamblichus.[54] Implicit in the answers (and often spread with apparent random across them) the modern reader can detect a clear systematic outline: *First*, there is discussion (1) of the nature of the gods and of the divine, then (2) of the nature of the human beings who offer sacrifice, and then (3) of the nature of the relationships between the humans and the gods/the divine. *Second*, what is taking shape, at least to modern eyes, is an overall theory of sacrifice, its nature and purpose, how and why it works, etc. *Third*, there is a discussion of the relationship between prayer and sacrifice. *Finally*, there is some discussion about divination and some attention to various false and simplistic ideas about sacrifice. In the course of all this, as one would expect from any Platonist serious about religion, Iamblichus has to deal with the problem of material and animal sacrifices offered to nonmaterial beings, to say nothing of the problem of the popular and often scandalously anthropomorphic traditional myths about the gods and their attitudes toward sacrifice.

---

[52] I am thinking most specifically of the *Mystagogic Catecheses* attributed to Cyril of Jerusalem (ca. 315–87 CE), and also delivered by, among others, Theodore of Mopsuestia, Ambrose, John Chrysostom, and Augustine. In Christian mystagogy, the mystagogue undertook to explain to the Christian neophytes the meaning and reality of what they had already begun to experience in their baptismal initiation rites.

[53] See Clarke, Dillon, and Hershbell, *Iamblichus* (above, p. 39, n. 50) 11.

[54] Ibid., xxii.

Everything starts, at least in terms of systematic logic, with Iamblichus's idea of the gods (*hoi theioi*) or the divine (*to theion*), terms which at times seem to be used interchangeably. But actually there are at least three or four different levels of beings that are being referred to with these terms. At the highest level is the supremely transcendent divine level, often described in such terms as "highest and most incomprehensible, superior to all measure, and formless in the sense of being unbounded by any form" (*DM* 1.7 [21]), or "the One, which is the supreme master of the multiplicity (of divinities)" (*DM* 5.22 [230]). Sometimes *to theion* seems to refer specifically to this highest level of Divinity, and not just to the general class of superior divine beings. At the next level are the gods/*hoi theioi*; beneath them are the daemons, and under them the heroes, and finally, under them, the souls, as Iamblichus spells out across Book 1 of the *DM*. All of this is relevant to the theme of sacrifice since each level of the divine that is being approached requires a correspondingly different level of theurgic ritual. While Iamblichus does not descend to the details of the rubrics, he does emphasize—as did pious pagans generally, for example, Symmachus at the end of the fourth century CE (see below, 2.12., pp. 49–50)—their overriding importance.

This concern for different levels of being also extends to his understanding of the human being (in modern terms, his anthropology). For Iamblichus first speaks of a "double status" of human beings, one the more exalted—and quite rare, he is careful to point out—when we have "become wholly soul," and "traverse the heights in company with all the immaterial gods," as opposed to being "confined in our hard-shelled body." This double mode of being human requires a "double mode of worship," and thus "two sorts of sacrifice," the one rare, "of men who are entirely purified," the other much more common (and necessary) of men who are "material and corporeal and based on alteration, as is suited to those still in the grip of the body.... Each person performs his cult according to the nature he has, not that which he does not have; one should not, therefore, overstep the measure proper to the sacrificing agent" (*DM* 5.15 [219–220]).

Shortly thereafter Iamblichus develops this further, now distinguishing between three rather than just two levels of human beings: First, there is the "great mass of men ... subject to the domination of nature ... ruled by natural forces" etc. Opposite them are a certain very few who "employing an intellectual power which is beyond the natural have disengaged themselves from nature" and such things, and finally there are some "who conduct themselves in the middle area between nature and pure mind" (*DM* 5.18 [223–24]). Iamblichus continues at great length, not giving the actual details of ritual worship, but stressing the vital importance of the principle that one must worship at and from the level at which one finds oneself, for it is only in that way that one can ascend from the lower and more material toward the higher and less material forms of worship. In page after page, especially from *DM* 5.21 and following, Iamblichus stresses, with a kind of neurotic scrupulosity, how complicated all this is and how important it is to get it exactly right—hence the need for theurgic experts—lest "the harmony and symmetry of the whole" (*DM* 5.21 [230]) be destroyed. In his own words, at the end of 5.21 [230]:

> He who leaves any [of the higher beings] without its share of honour subverts the whole, and wrenches asunder the unity of the total system; it is not a case, as one might think, of providing an imperfect reception, but of the absolute subversion of the whole rite.

The relatively brief Book 9 is devoted to "the personal daemon that presides over each one of us" (*DM* 9.9 [283]). These lower forms of divine being seem not unlike the guardian angels of traditional Christian piety, and they do have an important role in helping the human being toward the right forms of worship, for "when the personal daemon comes to be with each person, then he reveals the mode of worship proper to him and his name" (*DM* 9.9 [284]).

Having outlined Iamblichus's idea of the nature of the gods/the divine, and his idea of the nature of the human being, we can now attend more closely to his idea of the relationship between the divine and the human and, more specifically, to his concept of human destiny and, with that, his concept of the goal and purpose of the most important human theurgic activity, sacrifice. As we proceed, many readers may be surprised to discover how similar, not just analogous but also at times seemingly identical, is his thinking to that of the Christian Platonists, especially on the issue of the "divinization" of the human (see p. 85, n. 66).

At the very beginning of the work, Iamblichus's first reply to Porphyry makes some remarkable claims about the human-divine relationship that are foundational to his whole theurgic system: "An innate knowledge about the gods is coexistent with our nature, and is superior to all judgment and choice, reasoning and proof" (*DM* 1.3 [7]). Prior to that knowledge, which knows another as being itself other, there is a unitary connection with the gods that is natural... for it is rather the case that we are enveloped by the divine presence" (*DM* 1.3 [8]). This being "enveloped by the divine presence" is not metaphor but reality. For, in prayer, the gods "embrace within themselves the realizations of the words of good men, and in particular of those which, by virtue of the sacred liturgy, are established within the gods and united to them; for in that case the divine is literally united with itself" (*DM* 1.15 [47]). In this way, Iamblichus has, with this foundational insight, attempted to get around the problem of the presumed—for a Platonist—dichotomy between the human and the divine, the material and the immaterial.

At the end of Book 5, when addressing the issue of (theurgic) prayer and sacrifice, Iamblichus ties much of this together when he asks: "How would this not cast light on the final purpose of sacrifice (*to tōn thusion telos*), that is to say that it brings us into contact with the demiurge (*hōs sunaphēs kai auto dēmiourgikēs meteilēchen*), since it renders us akin to the gods through acts (*epeidē di' ergōn oikeiountai tois theois*)" (*DM* 5.26 [239-40]). Indeed sacrifices not only possess the capacity to connect us to the gods (*DM* 5.7 [207]), sacrificial rites are indeed the only means by which humans can enjoy participation with the higher beings (*DM* 5.23 [269]).

All of this has been introducing us to what moderns would call Iamblichus's general theory of sacrifice. Iamblichus himself opens this discussion for us in a passage that, whether intentionally or not, seems reminiscent of Theophrastus's list of the threefold purpose of sacrifice: to honor the gods, to thank the gods, and to ask for their help (see 2.3, pp. 29–32).

> I propose, then, to impart to you my views on sacrifices (*to ge emon dogma peri thusiōn*). These are that one should never indulge in them simply for the sake of conferring honour, in the way in which we honour our benefactors, nor in acknowledgement of races, in return for the good things which the gods have bestowed upon us, nor yet by way of first-fruits or a return of gifts, in recompense for the far superior gifts which the gods have provided for us; for all these procedures are common also to our dealings with men, and are borrowed from vulgar social relations, whereas they do not at all preserve the utter superiority of the gods and their status as transcendent causal principles. (*DM* 5.5 [206])

The very rhetoric or, indeed, the very "feel" of this passage alerts us that we are far, far beyond Theophrastus; for Iamblichus begins by exhorting us not to indulge in sacrifice simply for the three reasons briefly listed by Theophrastus. He devotes page after page to emphasize that sacrifice is far more profound and complicated than that. Although, he says, we have here "something of the truth and of the necessary consequences of sacrifices . . . there is still not demonstrated the true mode in which sacrifices operate" (*DM* 5.7 [208–9]). One must "seek the cause (of the efficacy of sacrifices) in friendship and affinity, and in the relation that binds together creators with their creations and generators with their offspring" (*DM* 5.9 [209]); for the goal is "one single bond of friendship, embracing the totality of beings, effecting this bond through an ineffable process of communion" (*DM* 5.10 [211]). For "the law of sacrifices is dependent upon the order of the gods themselves/*tēs tōn theōn taxeōs ton thesmon tōn thusiōn*"—*DM* 5.14 [217]), for ultimately, the goal, "the highest purpose of the hieratic art [is] to ascend to the One" (*DM* 5.22 [230]).

But how does this actually work? Or what is, as Iamblichus puts it, "the true mode in which sacrifices operate" (*DM* 5.7 [208])? He doesn't describe the rubrics, but he does go into considerable theoretical detail, beginning with the fact that "among the gods, some are material, others immaterial"; thus, "one must begin the sacrificial process from the material gods; for by no other route is ascent possible to the immaterial gods" (*DM* 5.14 [217]). The process being described here is clearly anabatic, from the material to the immaterial. But this is barely the half of it. After many pages of describing his complex ideas of theurgic worship, he also ends up emphasizing that what is transpiring is not just anabatic, but also, ultimately, and indeed originally, katabatic:

> The primary beings illuminate even the lowest levels, and the immaterial are present immaterially to the material. And let there be no astonishment if in this connection we speak of a pure and divine form of matter; for matter also issues—now quoting directly from Plato (*Tim.* 41a7 and *Pol.* 273b1)—"from the father and creator of all/*apo gar tou patros kai dēmiourgikou tōn holōn*." (*DM* 5.23 [222])

Iamblichus is thus thoroughly Platonistic in his sense that "nothing in the cosmic hierarchy depends on what is beneath it."[55]

---

[55] See Bradbury, "Julian's Pagan Revival and the Decline of Blood Sacrifice" (p. 39, n. 48) 340.

We have to remind ourselves that Iamblichus, for all his philosophical astuteness, is here presenting his *DM* at least to some extent as a faith document, at least in the sense that there are things that "require experience of actions," things therefore "that the uninitiated will not be able to understand."[56] As we have already pointed out (see p. 40, n. 52) this is not unlike what we find in the mystagogical catecheses of some of the Church Fathers like Cyril of Jerusalem a few decades later. It is even somewhat reminiscent of the way that St. Paul could speak of Christians offering their bodies as spiritual worship (*logikē latreia*) in Rom. 12:1, or of the spiritual body (*sōma pneumatikon*— 1 Cor. 15:44) of those who will rise from the dead. This manner of speaking makes no sense except to those already initiated in faith. In other words, whether one is an incarnational Christian or a Neoplatonic "mystagogue," one cannot speak about the mystery one is attempting to explain or proclaim without resorting to language that, while making sense to the initiated, in normal discourse can only seem to the uninitiated to be meaningless or involve logical inconsistencies.

It is, therefore, not surprising that Iamblichus concludes his main treatment of sacrifices by talking about prayer and sacrifice, and that this is the way in which he sums up his main teaching on the nature and purpose of sacrifice. He has begun this final section of his treatment of sacrifice (*DM* 5.26 [237–40]) by noting that it is specifically by prayers that sacrifices are brought to their "highest degree of completeness" that results in "an indissoluble hieratic communion with the gods," insisting that whether prayer precedes, accompanies, or concludes a sacrifice, "no sacred act can take place without the supplications contained in prayers—*ergon te ouden hieratikon aneu tōn en tais euchais hiketeiōn gignetai*" (*DM* 5.26 [238]). Prayer and sacrifice are, of course, not synonymous. Not all prayer involves sacrifice; but all sacrifice, apparently if it is to be considered true, proper, and effective, necessarily involves prayer, and specifically prayer of supplication, or, most specifically, "the supplications contained in prayers." Finally, he affirms that "the final purpose of sacrifice (*to tōn thusiōn telos*) . . . is . . . that it brings us into contact with the demiurge, since it renders us akin to the gods through acts

---

[56] See the second paragraph of Part 2.10, p. 40.

(*hōs sunaphēs kai auto dēmiourgikēs meteilēchen epeidē di' ergōn oikeiountai tois theois*)" (*DM* 5.26 [239–40]). For "sacrifice and prayer reinforce each other, and communicate to each other a perfect ritual and hieratic power" (*DM* 5.26 [240]). One might object that these English translations[57] make somewhat more explicit a meaning that may seem to be only implicit in Iamblichus's sometimes elliptical Greek prose. But that objection has force only if one takes these texts in isolation. In the context of Iamblichus's fairly extensive treatment of sacrifices and their place in his religious world, these translations clearly express his obviously intended meaning.

Finally, before leaving Iamblichus, here is a comment on why some of his theory of sacrifice seems to be similar to Christian thinking. Recent research suggests that some of the theology, demonology, and anthropology on which his thinking about sacrifice rests, "theology" that he apparently adapted from Porphyry, may have come from or by way of the Christian, Origen of Alexandria (see 3.3.o., pp. 95–96). Heidi Marx-Wolf writes, "In the third century, figures such as Origen, Porphyry, and Iamblichus refashioned the identity of the philosopher to include another facet, namely, ritual expertise and the access it gave to divinity."[58]

11 Sallust

Later, by the mid-fourth century, due apparently to the spread of Christianity and the increasing weakness of traditional Greco-Roman religion, to say nothing of the pro-Christian policies of most of the emperors, the practice of material sacrifice was in decline. The brief treatise of Sallust, *Concerning the Gods and the Universe*,[59] written probably in 363 CE in support of Julian the Apostate's pagan reform, and shortly before Julian's death, was probably a vain attempt to reverse the already beginning decline of paganism.[60]

---

[57] By Clarke, Dillon, and Hershbell, *Iamblichus* (see p. 39, n. 50).
[58] Marx-Wolf, "High Priests of the Highest God" (see p. 8, n. 15) 481–82.
[59] *Sallustius: Concerning the Gods and the Universe*, edited with prolegomena and translation by Arthur Darby Nock (Hildesheim: Georg Olms Verlagsbuchhandlung, 1996). This Sallust (or Sallustius) is to be distinguished from Sallust, the first-century BCE Roman historian and politician, and from Sallustius, the fifth-century CE cynic philosopher.
[60] Julian, "the Apostate" as the Christians called him (332–363 CE), gifted both intellectually and practically, and proponent of what one might call an enlightened paganism, was sole emperor for

Apparently influenced both by Julian's own writing and by the *De Mysteriis* of the Neoplatonist, Iamblichus, Sallust writes what amounts to a brief catechism of Hellenistic religion—which by that time amounts to Greco-Roman religion—in defense against Christianity's growing preeminence. His mention of "unbelief (*to atheias*) . . . in certain parts of the earth" (*Concerning the Gods* XVIII) seems to be a sad, resigned reference to Christianity.[61] Indeed, the very word *atheia* seems to be a borrowing from Christian writers. In a school-traditional way, Sallust appropriates the basic achievements of Greek religious philosophy and its characteristic, spiritualized understanding of *logikē thusia*. But along with that, in an impressive tour de force, he defends traditional material sacrifice, and specifically also animal sacrifice (*zōa thuousin anthrōpoi*) as actually consistent with that intellectual tradition. It was an unsuccessful rearguard action that, with the sudden death of the emperor Julian (Julian the Apostate, as Christians called him) came to naught. Perhaps this work never got published even in its own day, for there are no contemporary references to it. But we must let him speak for himself. In XIV he has already emphasized the common (literate-elite idea) that we do not affect or change the gods by our prayers and sacrifices; the effect is all in the good and the healing that takes place not in the gods but in us.[62] Note that the way he expresses this: *tēn hēmeteran kakian iōmenoi* (XIV—Nock p. 28) leaves open who the actual agent of this healing is.[63] Sallust proceeds,

> [XV] These considerations settle also the question concerning sacrifices and the other honours which are paid to the gods. The divine nature itself is free from needs; the honours done to it are for our good. The providence of the gods stretches everywhere and needs only fitness for its enjoyment. Now all fitness is produced by imitation and likeness. That is why temples are a copy of heaven, altars of earth, images of life (and that is why they are made in the likeness of living creatures), prayers of the intellectual element, letters of the unspeakable powers on high, plants

---

only the eighteen months following the death of Constantius in November 361. His untimely death in June of 363 allowed the still only incipient Christianization of the Roman Empire to resume without hardly missing a beat.

[61] Ibid., ci–civ.
[62] This, mutatis mutandis of course, is also a profoundly Christian insight, although admittedly, especially on the popular level, many Christians to this day have not risen to this level of insight.
[63] Ibid., 28.

and stones of matter, and the animals that are sacrificed [are a copy] of the unreasonable life in us. From all these things the gods gain nothing (what is there for a god to gain?), but we gain union with them. [XVI] I think it worth while to add a few words about sacrifices. In the first place, since everything we have comes from the gods, and it is just to offer to the givers first fruits of what is given, we offer first fruits of our possessions in the form of votive offerings, of our bodies in the form of hair, of our life in the form of sacrifices. Secondly, prayers divorced from sacrifices are only words, prayers with sacrifices are animated words, the word giving power to the life and the life animation to the word. Furthermore, the happiness of anything lies in its appropriate perfection, and the appropriate perfection of each object is union with its cause. For this reason also we pray that we may have union with the gods. So, since though [*sic*] the highest life is that of the gods, yet man's life also is life of some sort, and this life wishes to have union with that, it needs an intermediary (for objects most widely separated are never united without a middle term), and the intermediary ought to be like the objects being united. Accordingly, the intermediary between life and life should be life, and for this reason living animals are sacrificed by the blessed among men to-day and were sacrificed by all the men of old, not in a uniform manner, but to every god the fitting victims, with much reverence. Concerning this subject I have said enough. (XV–XVI, pp. 28–31)

Commentators point out that Sallust is not a profound original thinker, and that, for example, there is no evidence that he has more than just a passing, possibly only second-hand knowledge of the *De Mysteriis* of the gifted Neoplatonist, Iamblichus. Yet, in these two brief chapters of *Concerning the Gods* he has passed on to posterity—quite in contrast with the complicated claims of Iamblichus—perhaps the most helpful brief explanation of the nature and purpose of animal sacrifice to come from the world of classical paganism. To review his argument in modern terms, Chapter XV makes six points: (1) repeats the point made in XIV that the gods need nothing, and that prayers and sacrifices benefit only humans; (2) conflating the many distinctions found in Iamblichus, repeats the point that the gods (*hoi theioi*) and the divinity/ divine nature (*to theion*) are synonymous; (3) the benevolent providence of the divinity/the gods is universal and needs only fitness (*epitēdeiotēto*) for it to be enjoyed; (4) but all fitness is produced by imitation and likeness (*mimēsei kai homoiotēti ginetai*); (5) that is why temples are a copy of heaven, altars are copies of earth, images of life, etc., until finally the animals that are sacrificed (*ta de thuomena zōa*) are copies of the unreasonable life (*alogon zōēn*) in us; and (6) making an inclusion of the chapter, repeats point (1) and adds to it that what we specifically gain is union (*sunaphē*—Iamblichus's term) with the gods.

There is a wealth of meaning summed up in these two brief chapters: the nature of the divinity, including a benevolent providence whose benefits can be enjoyed via "fitness," which, in turn, is produced/achieved by imitation and likeness. Here Sallust is confronting one of the great weaknesses and challenges of the traditional Greco-Roman religion, namely, that it would never occur to any religious-minded intellectual to imitate the gods—especially the anthropomorphically imagined Olympian gods—while, at the same time, there is at least the vague general sense that blessedness/happiness/human destiny is somehow attained via imitation and likeness. That is why, ultimately, the animals (*ta zōa*) that are sacrificed are copies of the unreasonable life (*alogon zōēn*) in us. The upshot is, that while the gods gain nothing from all this, we gain union (*sunaphē*) with them.

The chain of the argument has its missing links, and much is left to the imagination to fill in. But it is overridingly clear that the purpose of sacrifice is for us to gain union with the gods/the divinity. Sallust seems to know that that is where his argument must end, presumably because, as he himself might well have sensed, only something as exalted as that can compete with the rhetoric of the Christians, and also because it seems to be what he has learned, whether directly or indirectly, from Iamblichus.

12 Symmachus

Toward the end of this brief sketch of Greco-Roman ideas about sacrifice, we come to the Roman statesman, orator, and man of letters, Quintus Aurelius Symmachus (ca. 345–402 CE). The contrast with Sallust is striking and, from the perspective of the now-open power struggle between Christian and Roman discourses about sacrifice, very revealing. Both Sallust and Symmachus argued for the preservation/continuance of the ritual practices of traditional

Roman religion including, but not necessarily emphasizing, animal sacrifice.[64] But their sense of why this was vitally important was tellingly different. For Sallust, like Iamblichus, the goal and purpose of sacrifice is union with the Divine, which union brings about our personal healing and well-being. For Symmachus, however, the goal and purpose of sacrifice, and of all the rituals of traditional Roman religion, was the health, the prosperity, and the good of the *res publica*. Sallust does not, of course, deny this specifically public goal and purpose of sacrifice, but he does not even mention it in his *Concerning the Gods*. It obviously did not rank high in his order of priorities. Looking back, we find the same relative lack of interest in the *De Mysteriis* of Iamblichus (see Part 2.10.). This internal difference—along with the fact that, except for Julian's brief reign (361–363 CE), all the emperors since Constantine favored the Christians—is probably a significant factor in explaining why the Christian story, or Christian sacrificial rhetoric, had, in the course of the fourth century, gained the upper hand.

The following paragraph sums up the situation at the turn of the fourth to the fifth century:

> This was the religious situation in Rome in the dying years of paganism: many-sided, contradictory, without any unifying bond. One had to choose from a bewildering arsenal to find the weapons needed to defend against an overwhelmingly advancing Christianity. Everyone knew who the common opponent was, but there was no unified basis of resistance. Should one be satisfied with a proud, but already withered tradition [e.g., Symmachus], or would the vitality of the mystery cults [e.g., those following Iamblichus] promise a more effective defense? Or would it be enough to set the rational system of the all-powerful Helios against the absolutizing claims of Christianity, and thus carry out the battle on the intellectual level? The leading minds of the time did not want to forgo any of these options. But whether one by one, or taken all together, Christianity seemed able, and eventually, by various means, to trump them all.[65]

---

[64] This lack of emphasis on animal sacrifice may well have been due to Symmachus's sensitive awareness of how revolting bloody animal sacrifice was to the (by then) increasingly numerous and influential Christians.

[65] Freely translated from: Richard Klein, *Symmachus: Eine tragische Gestalt des ausgehenden Heidentums*. Impulse der Forschung, Band 2 (Darmstadt: Wissenschaftliche Buchgesellschaft, 1971) 46.

13 Macrobius and the "end" of paganism[66]

At this time, or some decades later in the following century, Macrobius's *Saturnalia* indirectly witnesses to the extent of the Christian "victory." For if Macrobius is, as some argue, a pagan contemporary of Symmachus, the lack of urgency in the way in which he writes about sacrifice, in contrast to the worried urgency of Symmachus, is telling. But if, instead, he is a Christian writing about 430 CE, the matter-of-fact, unworried, and non-polemical way in which he writes about the various pagan practices of sacrifice—that is, as among the curiously antiquated, but no longer threatening, things that pagans used to do—is also telling.[67] Thus, whether Macrobius is a fourth-century pagan or a fifth-century Christian—history, though not decisively clear on this point, favors the latter option—the effect of the *Saturnalia* of Macrobius is to portray pagan sacrifice as, basically, a lost cause whose time is past.

---

[66] For general background, see 1.8., pp. 19–20, "The 'End' of Paganism?"
[67] As these remarks indicate, scholars are not sure who Macrobius was, or even precisely when he flourished. See Ambrosius, Aurelius Theodosius Macrobius, *Saturnalia*, ed. and trans. Robert A. Kaster, 3 vols., LCL 510–512 (Cambridge, MA/London: Harvard University Press, 2011) vol. 1, xi–xxiv. See also the chapter "Macrobius and the 'Pagan' Culture of His Age" in the massive magisterial work of Cameron, *The Last Pagans of Rome* (see above, p. ix, n. 3) 231–72.

Part Three

The Jewish-Christian Trajectory

Preliminary note: The many meanings of sacrifice[1]

I reported (in 1.5., pp. 11–13) on Kathryn McClymond's insistence that we look upon sacrifice in the ancient world as a "polythetic event," as a "dynamic matrix of activity" usually involving several, but not necessarily all, of the following seven activities: selection, association, identification, killing, heating, apportionment, and consumption.[2] That gave us a general history-of-religions descriptive definition of sacrifice to serve as a general background for Part 2. Here, as we begin Part 3, we are involved in a hermeneutical shift. My five decades of research that provides most of the background for what will be presented here was carried out from a largely unchallenged Christian perspective that now, however, is being brought into challenging conversation with my more recent study of sacrifice in non-Christian Antiquity.[3] Thus, as was already at least implicit from what has gone before, a traditional history-of-religions/historical-critical hermeneutic will now be working along with—and, I hope, in constructive tension with—a Christian theological hermeneutic. It is from the perspective of the latter hermeneutic that it may now be helpful to outline, as background, some six different meanings of sacrifice, any one of

---

[1] The substance of this "Preliminary note"—a temporary shift from primarily diachronic to primarily synchronic discourse—is taken extensively from my *Sacrifice Unveiled* (see p. viii, n. 1) 1–5 and my article "New Developments..." (see p. 17, n. 36).
[2] McClymond, *Beyond Sacred Violence* (see p. 4, n. 6) 29–33.
[3] There has, in fact, been little challenge to the fundamental perspective with which I have carried out my decades-long research into Christian sacrifice. But recently, Ullucci's *The Christian Rejection* (see p. 2, n. 3) has made me aware of a bias in that research: I came to it after an intensive study of sacrifice in Origen, which study gave me the perspective through and with which I, as the subtitle of *Christian Sacrifice* (see above, p. viii, n. 1) "The Judaeo-Christian Background before Origen" proclaims, read and interpreted the earlier data.

which, or almost any combination of which might be in play when someone in a modern or postmodern, but still Christian, context hears, reads, or uses the word "sacrifice."

1 General secular understanding of sacrifice

There is, first, a general secular understanding of the word: giving up something, usually something of at least some value, in order to get something of greater value. Because of the deprivation factor, there is inevitably some sadness or misfortune connected with it, and also, as we saw, even as early as Hesiod, some calculation too, in order to make sure that the good being obtained is of greater value than the good being given up. These secular, calculating—economic, if you will—and basically negative connotations of "sacrifice" are so pervasive and deep, so deeply rooted in the way we think and talk, that they inevitably influence almost all other uses of the word, even the most sublimely religious. It is not wise to pretend that they are not there.

2 General religious understanding of sacrifice

Here, sacrifice is generally understood as giving something valuable to God, often in a ceremony that symbolizes an internal offering of commitment or surrender to God, and in which an external gift is consumed or destroyed. Its purpose can be to acknowledge God's dominion, to seek for reconciliation with God or with the divinity that one may have offended, to render God thanks for blessings received or to petition for blessings still hoped for, and in general to establish, protect, or further the relationships that human beings have or want to have with the divine.

3 Sacrifice in the Hebrew Scriptures

What eventually became the Christian understanding of sacrifice was something that was already developing deep in the Old Testament, for example, in the accounts of the Genesis 4 sacrifices of Cain and Abel and the Genesis 8 sacrifice of Noah after the flood, namely, the vital importance of the sacrificer's religious dispositions, and the knowledge that God alone decides what an acceptable sacrifice is. But this divine decision was anything but arbitrary. As the prophets vigorously taught, it was connected with fulfilling the covenant requirements of justice and mercy. In addition, the (historical) connection, and for many (even to this day) the practical identification, of sacrifice with atonement has its roots deep in this biblical history. And finally, as Israel's religious sensitivity developed, there arose the awareness that what brought about atonement and communion with God was not precisely the performance of the sacrifice, but the fact that it was performed *in obedience to the Law*, that is, in accordance with God's will. This awareness developed into one of the singular religious achievements of late biblical and post-biblical Judaism: the belief that it was not ritual performance but prayer and the virtuous works of justice, mercy, and service that brought about or, speaking more accurately, occasioned reconciliation, atonement, and communion with God.

Christians must humbly recognize that they learned/inherited this insight from their Jewish forebears. This spiritualized—and for them now "Christologized"—idea of sacrifice is what Paul is preaching in Rom. 12:1: "Present your bodies as a living sacrifice, holy and acceptable to God, which is your spiritual worship." It is also what is at least implicitly intended in those several other New Testament passages[4] that speak about Christian sacrificial activity.

4 General Christian understanding of sacrifice

Christians understand that this offering can range all the way from something as transcendently precious as the heroic, self-giving dedication of one's life to the service of God, all the way down to something quite small like giving up some trivial pleasure for Lent. But Jesus' comments on the widow's tiny offering in Mk 12:43 and Lk. 21:3, not unlike what the pagan philosophers were already teaching, remind us that the value of an offering does not depend on its size; it depends rather on the extent to which what one does or offers is an aspect or expression of personal self-giving in union with Christ.

---

[4] Rom. 15:15–16; 1 Pet. 2:4–10; Heb. 10:19–25, 12:18–13:16.

5 Specifically Catholic understanding of sacrifice

The close relationship and, in the minds of many, the identity of the sacrifice of Jesus on the Cross and the Sacrifice of the Mass has been a central point of Catholic faith and teaching from the time of the Fathers of the Church right up to *Sacramentum Caritatis*, the recent (2007) post-synodal apostolic exhortation of Pope Benedict XVI. But this relationship has also been the focus of massive misunderstandings, by Catholics and Protestants alike, misunderstandings that have veiled rather than revealed the true nature of Christian sacrifice. Catholics and Protestants at the time of the Reformation agreed in seeing the New Testament as the fulfillment of the Old. Ironically (and fatefully) they also agreed in failing to recognize—as most theologians now do recognize—that the Christ-event, as Christian theology has come to understand and interpret it, had done away with sacrifice in the commonly understood history-of-religions sense of the word. Reformation-age Catholics and Protestants concurred, as many still do, in the same fatal methodological mistake of looking first to the religions of the world rather than to the trinitarian Christ-event in order to ascertain what it was that the early Christians were groping to express when, hesitatingly at first, because "sacrifice" was not what Christians did but what Jews and pagans did, they began to use sacrificial terms and images to refer to the death of Christ,[5] and to refer to the Eucharist, and eventually to refer also to their own Christian lives of self-giving love and service.

The practical identification of atonement with sacrifice that I mentioned above under *Sacrifice in the Hebrew Scriptures* exacerbated the consequences of these infelicitous ecumenical "agreements." Traditional Western atonement theory—at least in its extreme, but all-too-popular forms—ultimately reduces to something like the following caricature: (1) God's honor is damaged by sin; (2) God demanded a bloody victim to pay for this sin; (3) God is assuaged by the victim, Jesus; and (4) the death of Jesus the victim functioned as a payoff that purchased salvation for us. Such a theory is literally monstrous in some of its implications. For when it is absolutized—see Mel Gibson's film

---

[5] But note that the earliest followers of Jesus, along with most others living in the ancient Mediterranean world, would hardly have thought of the gruesome crucifixion death of Jesus as a sacrifice. See Ullucci, *The Christian Rejection* (p. 2, n. 3) 7–9.

The Passion of the Christ[6]—or pushed to its "theo-logical" conclusions and made to replace the Incarnation as central Christian doctrine, it tends to veil from human view, from Protestants as well as from Catholics, the merciful and loving God of biblical revelation.

Despite my books and articles on the subject, I had for many years lacked a satisfactory solution to this problem. That changed when, serendipitously asked to edit Edward Kilmartin's last (but at his death somewhat unfinished) book, I discovered therein—and indeed almost on its last page[7]—the trinitarian understanding of sacrifice to which I now turn.

6 Authentic Christian, that is trinitarian understanding of sacrifice

Constantly fine-tuning my own understanding of Christian sacrifice, I reproduce here, slightly augmented, the articulation of it that appears in the opening pages of *Sacrifice Unveiled*.

First of all, Christian sacrifice is not some object that we manipulate, nor is it something that we "do" or "give up." It is, first and foremost, a mutually self-giving event that takes place between persons. It is, in fact, the most profoundly personal and interpersonal event that we can conceive or imagine. It begins in a kind of first "moment," not with us but with the self-offering of God the Father in the gift-sending of the Son. It continues, in a second "moment," in the self-offering "response" of the Son, in his humanity and in the power of the Holy Spirit, to the Father and for us. And it continues further in a third "moment"—and only then does it begin to become Christian sacrifice—when we, in and by means of human actions that are empowered by the same Spirit that was in Jesus, begin to enter into that perfect, en-spirited, mutually self-giving, mutually self-communicating personal interrelationship that is the life of the Blessed Trinity.[8]

---

[6] Other modern films with a similarly faulty and negative understanding of sacrifice are Andrei Tarkovsky's (1986) *The Sacrifice* and Lars Trier's (1996) *Breaking the Waves*.
[7] Kilmartin, *The Eucharist in the West* (p. 3, n. 4) 381–82. Kilmartin's precise words, quite possibly written even as he lay dying, are, "Rather, sacrifice in the New Testament understanding—and thus in its Christian understanding—is, in the first place, the self-offering of the Father in the gift of his Son, and in the second place the unique response of the Son in his humanity to the Father, and in the third place, the self-offering of believers in union with Christ by which they share in his covenant relation with the Father."
[8] *Sacrifice Unveiled* (see above, p. viii, n. 1); the source of this trinitarian insight is Kilmartin, *The Eucharist in the West* (see p. 3, n. 4) 381–82.

This, in a nutshell, is the whole story. Everything else is just dotting the "i"s and crossing the "t"s. Anything less than this—that is, that is not at least beginning to become this—and most especially anything other than this, whether or not done by Christians, and however noble it might be, is simply not *Christian* sacrifice in the most authentic sense of the word.[9]

Transitional note[10]

Just as it was for the Greco-Roman religions of the ancient Mediterranean world, sacrifice was also the central religious institution of the ancient Israelites or, as Christians call them, the people of the Old Testament. The early Christians, after surviving those gnostic movements that tried to reject or prescind from this "Old" Testament, saw themselves as the "New Temple," or the "New Covenant." They began not only to refer to their own sacred writings as the "New Testament," but also to use sacrificial terms in talking about their founding event, the death and resurrection of Jesus Christ, thus appropriating for themselves the language, the imagery, and much of the rhetoric and implicit theology of the Jewish sacrificial system. No treatment of Christian sacrifice, and above all of sacrifice in Antiquity and Christianity, can ignore its background in the biblical religion of the Hebrews.[11] Part 3, "The Jewish-Christian Trajectory," for the most part and as will occasionally be noted, has been written in the awareness of the background and possible parallels already described in Part 2, "The Greco-Roman Trajectory."

1 The Hebrew Scriptures

The primary source for a history of Jewish ideas about sacrifice is, of course, the Hebrew Scriptures. But since these writings took shape over the course of the

---

[9] At the end of Part 3 in this book, "Excursus 3: A trinitarian view of sacrifice" (pp. 110–14), I summarize the evidence that allows us to claim that this trinitarian idea of sacrifice was, if not explicitly, then at least virtually and implicitly, present in the ancient Christian world.

[10] This is the point where we shift back from a primarily synchronic to a primarily diachronic mode of discourse, but also where the Origenian perspective that I noted above on p. 53, n. 3 in Part 3 comes into play.

[11] As Guy G. Stroumsa has powerfully argued in *The End of Sacrifice* (see p. 6, n. 12).

full millennium preceding the Christian era, and since they at times concern "events" that took place long before reports of or recollections of them were written down, and since these writings also underwent repeated revisions in which the attitudes and assumptions of the later redactors were projected back into the earlier events and accounts, it is no simple task to write—from our present vantage point another two millennia later—a critical history of early Israelite and subsequent later Jewish ideas about sacrifice. Space limitations require us to attend mostly just to the conclusions of the still ongoing research that necessarily lies behind such a critical history.

Assuming the correctness of the scholarly consensus regarding the sources of the Pentateuch—the first five books of the Bible were, in pre-critical tradition, thought to have been written by Moses—and assuming at least the basic validity of the source criticism that scholars for many decades have been applying to the whole of the Hebrew Bible, we can present some summary conclusions under the heading of two of the main types of sacrifice found in the Hebrew Scriptures: the burnt offering or holocaust, and the sin offering.

a. The burnt offering[12]

The burnt offering or "holocaust" (= "whole burnt offering") is the type of sacrifice most often mentioned in the Hebrew Bible; it is placed first in Israel's so-called Law of Sacrifice in chapters 1–7 of the book of Leviticus. It fulfilled a variety of functions and had a richness of meaning—adoration, praise, thanksgiving, atonement, petition, etc.—that later greatly influenced Christian ideas of sacrifice. In this type of sacrifice, the whole offering, whether animal or grain, was burned on the altar (see Leviticus 1 and 2). This distinguished it from offerings in which only part was burned on the altar with the rest being consumed by the people or by the priests (see Leviticus 3–5). This is what we find to be assumed in the accounts of the sacrifices of Cain and Abel (Genesis 4), of Noah after the flood (Genesis 8), and of Abraham almost sacrificing Isaac (Genesis 22). This is the type of sacrifice that, according to the earliest of the biblical books, had pride of place in most of early Israel's major feast-day celebrations.

---

[12] See Daly, *Christian Sacrifice* (p. viii, n. 1 in Foreword) 34–50.

b. Divine acceptance of sacrifice[13]

Closely associated with, but for the most part only implied, in the ceremony of the burnt offering, especially as Israelite religious understanding became more refined, was the "theology" of the divine acceptance of sacrifice. (But "theology," we have to remind ourselves, is a modern concept that we project back into our reading of ancient texts whose authors were more interested in practice than in theology or theory.) From the outset, the value or effectiveness of any sacrifice was understood to be wholly dependent on its acceptance by Yahweh. Behind this lay the common idea that accepting a gift bound the one receiving it to particular ties of favor to the giver of the gift. This is obvious, for example, in the reconciliation scene between Jacob and Esau in Gen. 33:9–11.

The most common Hebrew term used to express God's acceptance of a sacrifice, and thus God's approval and favor, was the Hebrew phrase "*reach nichoach*—pleasing odor/odor of sweetness." In the later biblical writings, this Hebrew phrase had become a wholly metaphorical reference to the divine acceptance of a sacrifice. But in the early, primitive use of this phrase, and in ways that are remarkably like similar ideas in ancient Greek religion, it referred to the pleasure of the gods (but in this case, Yahweh) in smelling the odor of a sacrifice. Obvious traces of this primitive meaning—the meaning so trenchantly satirized by the pagan, Lucian (see above 2.8., pp. 36–38)—are found in the account of the Lord's acceptance of Noah's sacrifice in Gen. 8:21 and in David's perplexed question in 1 Sam. 26:19 to King Saul who was seeking to kill him.[14] Literally, what David was saying to Saul was something like: "If perchance it is the Lord who has turned you against me, then may he be appeased by smelling an offering." Our modern translations, including even that of *The Jewish Study Bible*, do not translate the actual language of the metaphor, but only its metaphorical meaning.

---

[13] See Daly, *Christian Sacrifice, passim*; and *The Origins of the Christian Doctrine of Sacrifice* 21–25 (p. viii, n. 1).

[14] In Gen. 8:21: "And when the Lord smelled the pleasing odor." The typical modern translations of 1 Sam. 26:19 are, for example, in the *New Revised Standard Version*: "May he (the Lord) accept an offering"; in the *New American Bible*: "Let an offering appease him."

By the time of the third-century BCE Septuagint (abbreviated LXX) translation of the Hebrew Bible into Greek,[15] it had become clear that God's acceptance of a sacrifice was a totally free act. But, while God was never bound to accept anything, a properly offered sacrifice was somehow expected to effectively "reach" God. This involves the same paradoxical, apparent contradiction that religious thinking now associates with prayer. Proper prayer—in the minds of modern religious believers—like proper sacrifice—in the minds of ancient believers—is believed to be really effective, while God remains all the while totally free to answer or not to answer the prayer, or—more accurately it would seem—to answer it in ways that the petitioner does not expect or want. Thus, at this time, shortly before the end of the biblical era, the literate elites of the Israelite religion were in approximately the same "theological" place as were the more philosophically oriented literate elites of Greek religion: namely, divine acceptance was never automatic; the Divinity is free to accept or reject, and rejection is indeed a disaster.

However, there is a significant difference in what was happening in the biblical path of revelation in contrast to the more philosophical path of reason. The path of religion was revealing much more clearly to Israel, than the philosophers were figuring out for themselves, that God/the Divinity, while totally free and not subject to pressure, is nevertheless not arbitrary in dealing with human beings. At least, implicit in the acceptance or non-acceptance of even the early sacrifices of Cain and Abel in Genesis 4, but then, later, much more explicitly and powerfully preached by the Hebrew prophets than "figured out" by anyone in a non-Jewish or non-Christian context, is that the good conduct, and the ethical intentions and commitment of the offerer are of paramount importance in bringing it about that a sacrifice be actually "pleasing" or acceptable to God.

But the difference here can be seen as more one of degree than of total contrast. For the idea that the dispositions of the offerer are more important than the size of the offering was familiar to both the non-Jewish and non-Christian elite (see above 2.1. and 2.2., pp. 21–29); though, admittedly, it was not taught with the same force as Jesus' famous teaching about the "widow's mite" (Mk 12:41–44; Lk. 21:1–4) or with the same force as Jesus' remarkably pointed insistence in Mt. 5:23

---

[15] The Septuagint (LXX) translation of the Hebrew Bible into Greek, done in Alexandria in the third to second century BCE, was the authoritative translation through which the New Testament authors, and eventually most other early Christians, knew what they came to call the Old Testament.

that one must be reconciled with one's brother before approaching the altar to offer sacrifice—even to the point of interrupting an already-begun sacrificial ceremony—until this all-important requirement was met. Further heightening this degree of difference was the process of spiritualization in Judaism, subsequently inherited and deepened by Christianity, that was precipitated by the unique position and eventual unhappy fate of the Jerusalem Temple. For, well before the end of the biblical age, the Jerusalem Temple, had become, for religious Jews, the only place where one was allowed to offer the sacrifices that were absolutely necessary for atonement. By the dawning of the Christian era, and at least partly due to the Jewish experience of Exile, of Diaspora, and of the 70 CE destruction of the Temple, sacrifice in the Jewish tradition had come to be looked upon less and less as the precise performance of a material ritual act, and more and more as an act of obedience to the will of God. This opened the door, through which the Christians enthusiastically entered—and through which the Qumran sectarians, because of their estrangement from the Temple and priesthood of their day, had already been forced to enter—to the idea that the only true and effective act of sacrifice that is pleasing to God is not a ritual performed in a material temple, but rather the everyday—whether prosaic or heroic—fulfilling of the works of the Law, the doing of what God wants one to do, namely, prayer, almsgiving, fasting, good works, acts of reconciliation, teaching, healing, etc.

Excursus 1: "Leave your gift there before the altar" (Mt. 5:24)

In emphasizing, as we now should, the similarity between Jewish, pagan, and Christian ideas regarding the need for proper dispositions in the offering of sacrifice, this could lead us to overlook how radically revolutionary, even for some in our own day, was Jesus' teaching on the matter. Interrupting a sacred ritual, or leaving it unfinished, was something one just did not do. For it is at a particularly solemn point in Jesus' Sermon on the Mount that Matthew locates this teaching of Jesus. It is the beginning of the first of Jesus' solemn "you-have-heard-it-said . . . but-I-say-to-you" sayings:

> [21]You have heard that it was said to those of ancient times, "You shall not murder; and whoever murders shall be liable to judgment." [22]But I say to you

that if you are angry with a brother or sister, you will be liable to judgment; and if you insult a brother or sister, you will be liable to the council; and if you say, "You fool," you will be liable to the hell of fire. ²³So when you are offering your gift at the altar, if you remember that your brother or sister has something against you, ²⁴leave your gift there before the altar and go; first be reconciled to your brother or sister, and then come and offer your gift. (Mt. 5:21–24 [NRSV])

c. Sin offering and atonement[16]

The second type of ancient Jewish sacrifice we wish to highlight is the sin offering whose purpose was to achieve atonement for sin. Sin in the ancient Hebrew world was considered to be any act or offence—whether or not consciously committed—against a sacred ordinance, and hence against God and the majesty of God. Sin was never merely private but always, by its nature and especially in its effects, also a social reality. With Israel's intensely synthetic sense of life and of the interconnectedness of Temple, Land, and People, sin was seen as having let loose an evil and destructive force that, unless neutralized by atonement, would eventually wreak its havoc on the land and its people. Atonement can be described as the process whereby the originally positive creature-Creator relationship, after having been weakened, disturbed, or violated by the creature, is restored by the Creator to its proper harmony. Notice how similar this is to the thinking of some non-Christians, for example, the late-fourth-century Roman senator, Symmachus, that an important purpose of sacrifice is to maintain the *pax deorum* (see 2.12., pp. 49–50). After the sixth-century BCE Babylonian Exile and the restoration of the sacrificial cult in a rebuilt Jerusalem Temple—often referred to as the "Second Temple"—this process of atonement, although increasingly seen as an effect of all properly offered sacrifice, became especially identified with the sin offering.

In the process of atonement one can identify a positive and a negative function. The positive function is that of making persons or objects "acceptable" to Yahweh, of preserving them in this happy condition, and of making them eligible or preserving them as eligible to participate in Israel's

---

[16] See especially Leviticus 4 and 16, and Daly, *Christian Sacrifice* (p. viii, n. 1 in Foreword) 14–17, 25, 27, 31, 93–112.

religious life and cult. The negative—"apotropaic" it is often called—function is that of interrupting or averting the course of evil that had been set in motion by sin. But, what must be strongly emphasized, the agent of the atoning action, whether conceived of as positive or negative in function, was definitely not the human being, not the creature, but God, the Creator. What needs to be repeatedly emphasized is that what was most true to the actual content and above all to the most profound theological implications of the biblical witness, as this witness has been understood and interpreted by the best religious, exegetical, and theological minds of the Jewish and Christian traditions, is that *it is not the creature but God alone who is the actual agent of atonement*. It is true, however, that neither the Hebrew Scriptures nor the subsequent Jewish and Christian traditions, especially in the popular preaching and religiosity of these traditions, have always risen to and been faithful to this authentic understanding of atonement. The relative absence of this understanding among both the Protestants and the Catholics of that era seems to have been one of the enabling causes of the Protestant Reformation.

And in addition, especially worth highlighting is the following remarkable coincidence. After the Babylonian Exile and under the direction of the Jerusalem priesthood—in historical terms we are talking about the last four or five centuries before the Christian era—the regularly offered sin-offering ritual (see especially Chapter 4 of Leviticus) came to have the following seven parts or stages: (1) bringing to the altar the sacrificial material, an unblemished animal if those making the offering could afford it; (2) the ceremonial laying of hands on the animal victim, which signified some connection or identification—but definitely not penal substitution—between those making the offering and the animal victim; (3) the confession to the priests (see Lev. 16:21 and Mt. 5:23–24) in order to ascertain the purpose of the offering and assure the proper dispositions of those making the offering; (4) the slaughtering of the animal victim which was not—as has been commonly assumed—the high point of the sacrificial ceremony but simply the necessary means of obtaining the sacrificial flesh and sacrificial blood needed for the ceremony; (5) the blood rite, an action reserved to the priests; it was generally believed that atonement took place precisely in, during, or because of this rite; (6) a declaratory formula uttered by the priest(s), affirming that the sacrifice had been properly done and that God had accepted it and brought about the sought-for atonement; (7) the eating by the priests or the burning of the flesh of the sacrificial animal, the final act of the ritual. Especially worth the highlighting noted in the preceding two paragraphs, is how remarkably similar these seven aspects of the Hebrew sin offering are to the seven "activities" that, in various combinations, can be seen as constituting an action as sacrificial in pagan antiquity (see 1.5., pp, 11–13).

d. The blood rite and substitution[17]

The priestly manipulation of blood, whether by throwing, pouring, sprinkling, or smearing, was the high point of the sacrificial rite. As we have just indicated, this is the so-called moment, as nearly as that can now be discerned by us, at which atonement was thought to be taking place.

> We put "moment" in scare quotes in order to allude to the way in which Christians, especially in the West, have tended to fixate on the precise *moment* when something important takes place. E.g., precisely *when* does atonement (or the forgiveness of sins) take place? . . . precisely *when* does Christ become sacramentally present during the celebration of the Eucharist? . . . precisely *when* does someone become a priest during the ordination ceremony? . . . precisely *when* does an embryo become a human person? . . . precisely *when* do a man and woman become actually "man and wife"? and so forth.[18]

Four biblical passages or events stand out in giving witness to the centrality of the blood rite in Israelite history and religion: (1) The blood rite of the original (see Exodus 12) Passover in Egypt; (2) the book of Exodus' (24:3–8) unique covenant sacrifice in the desert. This was the people's ratification of Israel's formal, legal covenant relationship with Yahweh, and, incidentally, one of the rare times that Moses is described as performing the specifically priestly manipulation of sacrificial blood; (3) the atonement sacrificial rituals of the Leviticus 4 sin offering and the original Yom Kippur "event" in Leviticus 16; (4) finally, and most importantly, the prohibitions against any non-cultic use of blood in Lev. 17:11 and 14 and in Gen. 9:4. The single verse

---

[17] See Adalbertus Metzinger, "Die Substitutionstheorie und das alttestamentliche Opfer mit besonderer Berücksichtigung von Lev. 17,11," *Biblica* 21 (1940) 159–87, 247–72, 353–77; Notker Füglister, "Sühne durch Blut—Zur Bedeutung von Leviticus 17,11," in Georg Braulik, *Studien zum Pentateuch* (Vienna/Freiburg/Basel: Herder, 1977) 143–64; Daly, *Christian Sacrifice* (p. viii, n. 1 in Foreword) 87–136.

[18] But asking about the precise moment when atonement takes place is a modern question—and perhaps especially a modern "Catholic" question, analogous to Catholic concern about the "moment of consecration" of the Eucharist—that apparently was of much less concern to those in Antiquity.

Lev. 17:11 can be described as Israel's most central and sacred divine ritual ordinance. In the NRSV version it reads:

> For the *life* of the flesh is in the blood; and I have given it to you for making atonement for your *lives* on the altar; for, as *life* (*b^enephesh*), it is the blood that makes atonement. (Lev. 17:11)

Behind each of the three italicized English words in this text, *life, lives, life*, is the same Hebrew word: *nephesh*. Its massive range of meaning, all of it at least implicitly in play here, includes *soul, living being, life, self, person, desire, appetite, emotion, passion*, etc. Thus, with blood identified with life, and with the Lord alone acknowledged as having sole dominion over life, this divine decree is declaring that the only use to which blood can be put is in the ritual act of "making atonement for your lives on the altar."

There is, it needs to be emphasized, no suggestion of substitution in this Hebrew text. However, substitution is clearly suggested by its third-century BCE Septuagint (LXX) Greek translation, the translation most familiar to the Greek-writing authors of the New Testament and revered by early Christians as the inspired Word of God. There, the Hebrew *b^enephesh* is translated, in the same way as the *lex talionis*—"eye for an eye"—as *anti tēs psychēs/in place of the soul*, instead of the more precise *as life* (as translated in both the Jewish Study Bible and the New Revised Standard Version). It was largely because of this massive mistranslation, this insertion of explicit substitutionary meaning into so key a text, that so many have assumed that the Bible teaches a substitutionary idea of sacrifice. Jerome, who actually knew enough Hebrew to know better, and despite his own self-proclaimed allegiance to the "*veritas Hebraica*," perpetuated this error in his (eventually) authoritative late-fourth-century Vulgate translation of the Bible into Latin. His translation of the last half of Lev. 17:11, *ut super altare in eo expietis pro animabus vestris, et sanguis pro animae piaculo sit* (literally: "that it might there on the altar make expiation for your souls, and the blood be a sin offering for the soul") is more a translation of the Greek Septuagint with its mistaken substitutionary meaning than a faithful rendering of the original Hebrew.[19]

---

[19] Both of the early-seventeenth-century authoritative English translations, the Catholic Douay-Rheims Bible (*and the blood may be for an expiation of the soul*) and even more strongly the

There were, to be sure, a number of reasons why, as one approached the Christian era, ideas associated with substitution were in the air. There was the annual celebration of Israel's firstborn being "redeemed/spared" by the blood of the Passover lambs; there were the unforgettable remembrances of Abraham interceding for Sodom (Gen. 18:22–33), and of Moses interceding for the people (Exod. 32:30–32), and later of David doing the same (2 Sam. 24:17). There was the idea of a just man atoning vicariously for Israel as in the Servant Songs of Isaiah (Isa. 42:1–4, 49:1–6, 50:4–11, 52:13–53:12). In addition, the martyrdom texts of the Second and Fourth Books of Maccabees are clear pre-Christian sources for the idea of vicarious and even atoning suffering. See especially the prayer of Eleazar in 4 Mac. 6:28–29: "Be merciful to your people, and let our punishment suffice for them. Make my blood their purification, and take my life in exchange for theirs." In the late biblical period, ideas of substitution were obviously in the air and obviously feeding into what the late Jewish and early Christian mind and imagination was "finding" as it read/heard the Bible.

e. From the Old Testament to the New Testament[20]

As we approach the Christian era, the question becomes more pressing: what are the possible connections between nascent Christianity and non-Christian Antiquity? The answer begins with the observation that the original matrix of Christianity was not precisely the Hebrew Scriptures, but rather the religious Judaism of the post-biblical, intertestamental period. Religious Judaism had already been in significant contact with Greek culture ever since at least the third-century BCE Alexandrian translation of the Hebrew Scriptures into the Greek Septuagint (LXX), and in a state of obvious conflictual contact since the Maccabean revolt against the attempted imposition of Greek culture under Antiochus Epiphanes IV in 167 BCE. In addition, most of the late biblical or post-biblical Jewish writings were written not in Hebrew or Aramaic but in Greek. The New Testament and all of the now extant early Christian writings

---

Protestant King James Bible (*for it is the blood that maketh atonement for the soul*) emphasize this mistaken substitutionary meaning.

[20] See Daly, *Christian Sacrifice* (p. viii, n. 1) 139–207; and *The Origins of the Christian Doctrine of Sacrifice* (also p. viii, n. 1) 36–52.

were also composed in Greek, the lingua franca of the ancient Mediterranean world, the language not just of Plato and Aristotle but also, except for Latin-speaking North Africa, of most of the literary elites of Antiquity, Christian as well as pagan, until well into the Roman imperial period.

f. Qumran and the Dead Sea Scrolls[21]

The sectarian Jewish community that produced the Qumran writings, the Dead Sea Scrolls, did not participate in the sacrificial cult of the Jerusalem Temple. The Qumran community considered the Temple to have been defiled and its priests to be illegitimate.[22] Instead, in the Qumran writings, prayer took the place of sacrifice and was considered to be better than the impure sacrifices in the Temple.[23] One result of this is that the Qumran writings show a close relationship between sacrifice and the language of prayer.[24] However, the precise relationship between sacrifice and prayer in the so-called "sectarian" Qumran writings is in dispute among scholars.[25] There are three major positions: (a) prayer is understood as a replacement for the sacrifices that are necessary for atonement but now impossible to carry out in the Jerusalem Temple;[26] (b) prayer, while not a replacement for sacrifice, does correspond to a "communal act of righteousness that has atoning significance";[27] (c) the replacement of sacrifice by prayer is only a temporary solution, as long as no sacrifice in the Temple is possible.[28] This third understanding seems to be

---

[21] See Daly, *Christian Sacrifice* (p. viii, n. 1) 157-74; and *The Origins of the Christian Doctrine of Sacrifice* (also p. viii, n. 1) 44-47. In addition, this section is a translation/modified adaptation of what was originally written by Theresa Dockter (née Nesselrath) in the *RAC* 26.167-69 (see p. viii, n. 1 and n. 2).

[22] For example, see CD (the Qumran Damascus Document) 6.11-14, 20, 21, and Joseph M. Baumgarten, "Sacrifice and Worship among the Jewish Sectarians of the Dead Sea [Qumran] Scrolls," *Harvard Theological Review* 46 (1953) 144-45.

[23] For example, CD 11.18-21.

[24] Francesco Zanella, *The Lexical Field of the Substantives of "Gift" in Ancient Hebrew* (Leiden: Brill, 2010) 123-26, 160-62, 311-13, 412-13; "minhah" in *THWbQumran* 2 (2013) 716.

[25] For an overview: Zanella, "The lexemes teruma and mana in the Poetic Texts of Qumran," in Armin Lange, Emanuel Tov, and Matthias Weigold, eds., *The Dead Sea Scrolls in Context*, vol. 1 (Leiden: Brill, 2011) 160-62.

[26] For example, Georg Klinzing, *Die Umdeutung des Kultes in der Qumrangemeinde und im Neuen Testament* (Göttingen: Vandenhoeck & Ruprecht, 1971).

[27] Russell C. D. Arnold, "Qumran Prayer as an Act of Righteousness," *Jewish Quarterly Review* 95 (2005) 512.

[28] Eileen M. Schuller, "Worship, Temple and Prayer in the Dead Sea Scrolls," in Alan J. Avery-Peck, Jacob Neusner, and Bruce Chilton, eds., *Judaism in Late Antiquity* 5 (Leiden, 2001) 125-43; Daniel K. Falk, "Prayer in the Qumran Texts," in William Horburg, William D. Davies, Louis Finkelstein,

the most likely since, for example, 1QM (the *War Scroll*) 2.1–6 describes the sacrifices that will again take place in the Temple in eschatological time after the victory of light.[29] There aren't many biblical models for the replacement of material sacrifice with prayer or praise. Yes, the oft-recited Ps. 141(140):2 does seem to speak of an equivalence between sacrifice and prayer: "Let my prayer rise before you like an incense offering; my uplifted hands an evening sacrifice." However, despite the frequency of this verse in later Christian prayer, in the Bible itself it is something of an exception.

Qumran's replacing of the sacrificial cult with prayer or praise is shown very clearly in 11 QPs^a 18.7–9 (on Ps. 154:10–11) where we read: "Whoever praises the Most High will be accepted by him exactly like someone who offers sacrifice."[30] In this process of spiritualization there thus developed an understanding of the community as the New Temple. The so-called *Community Rule* (1QS) contains indications that, instead of the Temple, the community itself became increasingly the place where atonement took place. In fact, the community itself came to be understood as sacrifice.[31] 1QH 6.26 and 4QFlor 1.6–7 express themselves similar to the way in which 1 Pet. 2:4–10 (see 3.2.*d.4.*, pp. 77–78) later spoke of building up a Temple of people instead of stones.[32] The texts found in Qumran thus express a strong symbolic understanding of the Temple: the community of Qumran is itself the New Temple; sacrifice is something purely spiritual that is offered by a holy and pure way of life as well as by the praise and prayer of the community.[33] For more detail on the idea of a heavenly liturgy, or of a liturgy celebrated in common with angels, see Daly, *Christian Sacrifice* (see p. viii, n. 1) 171–74.

Steven T. Katz, and John Sturdy, eds., *The Cambridge History of Judaism* 3 (Cambridge: Cambridge University Press, 1999) 852–76.

[29] See Daly, *Christian Sacrifice* (p. viii, n. 1) 171; cf. 1 QpHab 8.8–13; Baumgarten, "Sacrifice and Worship" (p. 68, n. 22) 142.

[30] Zanella, "Minhah" (p. 68, n. 24) 717. Similar ideas are also found in Rabbinic Judaism (jBerakot 8b; bMenahot 110a; bBerakot 15a; bSanhedrin 43b.

[31] 1QS 3.6–12; 5.4–7; 8.5–10 (the Council of the Community as the Holy of Holies: *qodes qodasim*); 9.3–6; Daly, *The Origins of the Christian Doctrine of Sacrifice* (see p. viii, n. 1) 45–46; idem, *Christian Sacrifice* (see p. viii, n. 1) 160–69; regulations regarding animal sacrifice are not found there at all; Baumgarten, "Sacrifice and Worship" (p. 68, n. 22) 149.

[32] Daly, *Christian Sacrifice* (see p. viii, n. 1) 166–69; 257–59.

[33] Bertil E. Gärtner, *The Temple and Community in Qumran and the New Testament* (Cambridge: Cambridge University Press, 1965) 16–46; Baumgarten, "Sacrifice and Worship" (p. 68, n. 22) 149–50.

Excursus 2: Spiritualization

Having seen how the Qumran sectarians, unable to participate in the sacrificial ritual of the Jerusalem Temple, spiritualized their understanding of the sacrifices that their faith tradition told them were necessary for atonement; and since that Qumran experience contains "the single most important non-biblical source for the background of the early Christian idea of sacrifice,"[34] it may be helpful to clarify what we mean by "spiritualization." One can begin by listing a few synonyms: *dematerializing, sublimating, humanizing, deepening, ethicizing, rationalizing, interiorizing, symbolizing, metaphoricizing,* and so forth. But no one of these is adequate, and some, like "*dematerializing*," can be misleading, undercutting, as it does, the incarnational thinking of the Christians and their commitment to the inner, spiritual, or ethical significance of sacrifice. Yes, the various meanings of "spiritualization" contain or imply some shift in emphasis from the material to the spiritual, but, for a true Christian, never to the extent of radically derogating the material or the bodily. Convinced Christians could never forget that God had come to them, born of Mary, *in the flesh* and that, as Paul put it in Rom. 12:1, they had been called to offer their *bodies* as spiritual—that is, "Christic" worship. Thus, our use of the words "spiritualize" or "spiritualization" does not imply the narrowly anti-material, anti-institutional sense often attributed to them by critical scholarship.

2 The Christian Scriptures (New Testament)

Paul's words *logikē thusia* in Rom. 12:1 betray at least some familiarity with Greek religious thinking on sacrifice. However, such borrowing, if that is what it was, apart possibly from Paul's use of the words "*leitourgos*" and "*leitourgei*" a few chapters later in Rom. 15:16, is not found elsewhere in the NT. Thus, in terms of sacrifice, early Christianity's engagement with its ambient culture seems to have been at first primarily with Judaism, and then only later with the rest of Antiquity.

---

[34] See Daly, *The Origins of the Christian Doctrine of Sacrifice* (see p. viii, n. 1 in Foreword) 44.

The statement (from ca. 54 CE) by the earliest recorded Christian writer, Paul, "For our paschal lamb, Christ, has been sacrificed [*kai gar to pascha hēmōn etuthē Christos*]" (1 Cor. 5:7), places Christ at the center of the most foundational of Jewish (and, subsequently, Christian) feasts. Significantly, despite the relative uniqueness of the statement, its context—basically a throwaway statement apparently needing no explanation—suggests that this was not a new or strange idea for the Corinthians. And this is hardly the only instance of Christians fairly early appropriating Jewish sacrificial language and imagery. Equally striking, upon reflection, is the Christian remembrance of the eucharistic words of Jesus at the Last Supper, at what many regard as the "moment" of the institution of the central Christian sacrament: "This is my blood of the covenant, which is poured out for many" with the Matthaean version adding "for the forgiveness of sins," thus totally—outrageously for Jewish sensitivities—appropriating for Christian purposes the uniquely foundational Hebrew covenant sacrifice of Exod. 24:3–8.[35]

a. Lack of liturgical-historical data

However, when we try to unpack the first few centuries of Christian liturgical history in order to be more precise about the actual history of the possible relationships between Christianity and its ambient cultures, we are at an impasse. We simply don't have enough data to write such a history. But the data we do have undercuts the common assumption that most Christian scholars, until recently, have been bringing to this study, the assumption that if we had enough data, we could draw a clear line of development from the actions of Jesus at the Last Supper up to the developed theology undergirding the elegant Christian liturgies and Eucharistic Prayers of the patristic golden age some four centuries later. The available historical data actually suggests just the opposite, that is, that there was great plurality rather than unity in early Christian liturgical practice, and that the closer

---

[35] Mk 14:22–25 at 24; Mt. 26:26–29 at 28. See also Lk. 22:15–20 and 1 Cor. 11:23–26. The shape of these remembered eucharistic words of Jesus, with their similarities and differences, show (to modern scholars) obvious signs of the liturgical formation of these words that was taking place in the time (some twenty-five years for Paul; some four or five decades for the gospel writers) between the historical Last Supper and these words being recorded in the New Testament.

one moves back to the time of the historical Jesus, the more diverse and plural is the practice that one finds.[36]

For our purposes, the best we can do is attempt to summarize the extent to which, in its first centuries of existence, the early Christians, but not necessarily in any unified or even consistent way, seemed to be not only appropriating Jewish sacrificial language and imagery but also, de facto if not by conscious plan, to be constructing the rhetoric of the power of sacrifice[37] that, in the ensuing centuries, they would use to great effect not only against pagan sacrificial rhetoric, but also against the other eventual "losers" among the various Christian groups striving for supremacy.

b. Acts of the Apostles

Written probably between 80 and 90 CE, some three, four, or five decades after the actual events it narrates, the book of Acts contains an ambiguous record about the attitude of the earliest followers of Jesus toward the sacrificial cult of the Jerusalem Temple. Early in Acts we read: "They spent much time together in the temple, . . . and having the goodwill of all the people" (Acts 2:46–47). Then, in the following early chapters of Acts, recounting the increasing conflict of the Apostles with the Jewish authorities, there is no indication that the conflict concerned the sacrificial ritual. Nor is there much suggestion of such conflict in the rest of Acts, especially the account in Acts 21:15–26 that describes Paul's conformity to the Law in taking a temporary Nazirite vow that involves an act of sacrifice. On the other hand, that initial favorable attitude toward Temple and sacrifice was countered in Acts 6 and 7. Stephen, accused of "saying things against this holy place" (Acts 6:13), defends himself with a lengthy traditional account of salvation history from Abraham up to Solomon who "built a house" (Acts 7:47) for God. But with that comment Stephen launches into an aggressive attack: "The Most High does not dwell

---

[36] See Robert J. Daly, S.J., "Eucharistic Origins: From the New Testament to the Liturgies of the Golden Age," *Theological Studies* 66 (2005) 3–22; Paul F. Bradshaw, *The Search for the Origins of Christian Worship*, 2nd ed. (New York/Oxford: University Press, 2002); idem, *Eucharistic Origins* (New York/Oxford: University Press, 2004); idem, *Reconstructing Early Christian Worship* (Collegeville, MN: Liturgical Press, 2010). See the recent updating of much of this research in Andrew B. McGowan, *Ancient Christian Worship: Early Church Practices in Social, Historical, and Theological Perspective* (Grand Rapids, MI: Baker Academic, 2016).

[37] See Heyman, *The Power of Sacrifice* (p. 6, n. 12).

in houses made with hands—en cheiropoiētois" (7:48), thus referring to the temple, as Jesus in Mk 14:58 is recorded as doing at his trial, as something "made with hands," the traditional Jewish polemical term used to describe idols. The result of seeming to call the temple an idolatrous human work is the same for Stephen as it was for Jesus at his trial: enraged condemnation and execution.

Acts does enable us to construct at least a general—even if selectively idealized—picture of the early decades of Christianity, but the ambiguity regarding primitive Christian attitudes toward the sacrificial worship of the temple remains. The persistence, or recurrence, of the charge against Stephen, described by the narrator as coming from false witnesses, but then apparently proven to be true by Stephen's own words, is significant. For the same kind of charge not only reminds us of Jesus' trial, it is also made against Paul at the very time when he, apparently in good faith, is participating in a sacrificial act: "This is the man who is teaching everyone everywhere against our people, our law, and this place" (Acts 21:28). Thus, whether with accurate historical recollection, or perhaps only projecting late-first-century Christian-Jewish antipathy back into the earlier years, Acts at times portrays Jews as seeing Christians as opposed to the temple and its sacrifices. But at other times, and more consistent with our best reconstructions of the first few Christian decades, Acts also portrays the earliest followers of Jesus as continuing to take part in Jewish temple sacrifice.

c. The gospels

This apparent ambiguity is more or less confirmed by the witness of the Christian gospels written, for the most part, in the last quarter of the first century, and thus, at a time of already established Christian-Jewish antipathy. There are texts that assume a basically favorable attitude toward the Jewish sacrificial cult. For example, Mt. 5:23-24, insisting that one be reconciled with one's brother before offering sacrifice—see our treatment of this above, pp. 62-63—makes sense only under such a favorable supposition. The same supposition is implied in Jesus' instruction to the healed leper to "show yourself to the priest" (Mk 1:40-44; Mt. 8:1-4; Lk. 5:12-14). But there are also texts, such as Jesus' inflammatory "not-made-with-hands" remark at his trial in Mk 14:58, that seem to make sense only in the context of a strong anti-cultic, anti-sacrificial attitude. And there are numerous texts that really are ambiguous, such as Jesus' cleansing of the temple, one of the very few pre-passion events recorded in each of the four gospels (Mk 11:15–19; Mt. 21:12–13; Lk. 19:45–48; Jn 2:13–17). Was Jesus attempting, as others had also attempted,[38] merely to purify the temple for more proper sacrificial activity? Or was his action a substantial threat to that activity?

d. Paul and the Epistles[39]

When we look at the Epistles, written mostly in the forties and fifties well before the gospels, we find a different kind of ambiguity. The ambiguity of the gospels stems partly from their genre as faith-historical documents written mostly *after* the 70 CE destruction of the temple but *about* events that took place several decades earlier when Jewish temple sacrifice was in full flower, but written *for Christians* for whom temple sacrifice was no longer possible, necessary, or even desired. On the other hand, the ambiguity from the authentic Pauline Epistles comes from the fact that they are written at a time when the only-at-Jerusalem Temple sacrifices were still being practiced, but were written from and to places distant from Jerusalem, and to people who were mostly non-Jewish—or at least no longer Jewish—Christians, as they were beginning to be called, living in contexts and cultures in which pagan sacrifice was taken for granted as part of the culture in which they were living, but in which culture, at least in its overtly sacrificial aspects, they, as Christians, did not participate. In these letters we find not only what modern readers find to be an at least implicit rejection of Jewish sacrifice along with an obvious explicit rejection of pagan sacrifice, but also, along with all that, an extensive Christian appropriation of Jewish sacrificial language and imagery.[40]

---

[38] See Bruce Chilton, *The Temple of Jesus: His Sacrificial Program within a Cultural History of Sacrifice* (University Park: Pennsylvania State University, 1992) 91–111.

[39] See Daly, *Christian Sacrifice* (p. viii, n. 1) 230–95; and *The Origins of the Christian Doctrine of Sacrifice* (also p. viii, n. 1) 59–78.

[40] This sacrificial language and imagery was basically that of the authoritative-for-Christians Septuagint (LXX) Greek translation of the Hebrew Bible. The terminology is recognizably similar to, but often with significant little changes from, the way pagans spoke and wrote about sacrifice. These "significant little changes" were apparently important for the way in which the early Christians could be seen not as totally rejecting sacrifice but as spiritualizingly reinterpreting sacrifice in order to use its language and imagery to express their self-understanding of their own Christian lives. For example, instead of the normal Greek *holokautēsis* for "holocaust," the Septuagint would use

That appropriation allows Paul and the other writers of the NT Epistles to articulate at least the framework of what, a few centuries later, became a remarkably full and specifically Christian theology of sacrifice.[41] It has three main themes: (1) the sacrifice of Christ, (2) Christians as the New Temple, and (3) sacrifice of (i.e., by) Christians.

1 The sacrifice of Christ

We have already seen how Paul, hardly more than two decades from the actual time of Christ, witnesses how the Corinthian Christians could think of Christ (presumably Christ crucified) as their paschal sacrifice: "Our paschal lamb, Christ, has been sacrificed" (1 Cor. 5:7). Further, in two other places Paul speaks of Christ as a sin offering: "He [God] made him [Christ] to be *sin* [i.e., a sin offering] who knew no *sin*" (2 Cor. 5:21; see also Rom. 8:3). The italicized *sin* translates the Greek *hamartia* that, in turn, is the usual Greek translation for the Hebrew *chattat*, a word that meant both "sin" and "sin offering/sacrifice for sin." Paul seems to have been consciously playing on this double meaning. However, as Ullucci argues (*Christian Rejection* [see p. 2, n. 3] 6–9) and as many others have pointed out, no one in Christ's time would have thought of his death on the cross as a sacrifice. It was a horribly painful and degrading execution. If Paul had really wanted to argue that it was a sacrifice, he would not have done so with just these brief "one-liners." But, on the other hand, it is also significant that Paul's listeners/readers were apparently not upset by the sacrificial implications of these statements.

2 Christians as the New Temple

We do not know whether Paul knew the work of his contemporary, the Greek-writing Philo of Alexandria, who spoke of the individual soul as an altar.[42] Nor do we know whether Paul was influenced by the community-as-temple ideas contained in the Dead Sea Scrolls from Qumran.[43] We have no direct evidence

---

holokautōsis, changing just one vowel—*ē* to *ō*—to alert the reader/hearer that this was not a normal pagan holocaust. See Suzanne Daniel, *Recherches sur le vocabulaire du culte dans la Septante*, Études et Commentaires 11 (Paris: C. Klincksieck, 1966).

[41] My recent engagement with Ullucci's *The Christian Rejection* (see p. 2, n. 3) has made me aware that, in my previous research, I myself had to some extent been reading back into Paul the fullness of Origen's (ca. 185–ca. 251 CE) theology of sacrifice.

[42] See 3.3.i., pp. 87–89.

[43] See Daly, *Christian Sacrifice* (p. viii, n. 1) 157–74.

to settle such questions. But in any case, he clearly tells the Corinthians: "You are God's temple."[44]

3 Sacrifice of/by Christians

In numerous texts, Paul and the other NT Epistle writers compare and even identify the life and death of Christians with the (sacrificial?) death of Christ.[45] These texts show that Paul viewed his own apostolic life and impending death in the same way that he viewed Christ's, that is, as a personal self-offering. This is what he is summing up when he writes:

> I appeal to you, therefore, brothers and sisters, by the mercies of God, to present (*parastēsai*) your bodies (*sōmata*) as a living sacrifice holy and acceptable to God, which is your spiritual (*logikēn*) worship. Do not be conformed to this world, but be transformed by the renewing of your minds, so that you may discern what is the will of God—what is good and acceptable and perfect. (Rom. 12:1–2)

This also seems to be what he is referring to when, a few chapters later, he writes,

> Because of the grace given me by God to be a minister (*leitourgos*) of Christ Jesus to the Gentiles in the priestly service (*leitourgein*) of the gospel of God, so that the offering of the Gentiles may be acceptable and sanctified by the Holy Spirit. (Rom. 15:15–16)

We have here already the outline of what later Christians could hear and read as the beginning of a remarkably full theology of Christian life as sacrificial comprising (1) the offering up of Jesus Christ, to God, and for us, (2) the "priestly [i.e., sacrificial] service" of a life of living and preaching the gospels, and (3) the obedience of faith in giving oneself to God for the sake of one's neighbor.[46] Paul's description of this sacrifice as *logikēn*, instead of what was

---

[44] 1 Cor. 3:16; see also 1 Pet. 2:5–10 and the deutero-Pauline Eph. 2:19–22.
[45] Rom. 8:36; 2 Cor. 4:10–11; Gal. 2:19–20; Col. 1:24. It should be noted that these texts, taken strictly in their own context, are at best only implicitly sacrificial. But, as read and experienced by later Christians, they are profoundly sacrificial.
[46] On the *logikē thusia* theme, see Philipp Seidensticker, *Lebendiges Opfer (Röm 12,1): Ein Beitrag zur Theologie des Apostels Paulus*, Neutestamentliche Abhandlungen 20. 1/3 (Münster i. W.: Aschendorff, 1954) 1–43, and also the major commentaries on this passage, for example, Ernst Käsemann, *An die Römer* (Tübingen: Mohr, ⁴1980) 313–19, 378–79; Otto Michel, *Der Brief an die Römer* (Göttingen: Vandenhoeck & Ruprecht, ⁴1966) 290–93, 364–65; Heinrich Schlier,

for Christians the more common *pneumatikēn*—a word that evokes "Holy Spirit" instead of just "spirit" in general—indicates at least some familiarity with Greek philosophical thinking about sacrifice.

4 1Pet. 2:4-10

This passage is the richest single source for a New Testament theology of sacrifice.[47] It explicitly takes up and amplifies the Pauline idea of the community as temple, and does so in ways that are analogous to, and perhaps even influenced by, the Qumran idea of the community as temple (see 3.1.f., pp. 68-69). It also proclaims the sacrificial nature of Christian life, while implicitly holding in the background the idea of the sacrifice of Christ. The first two verses of this passage are the richest two verses for a biblical theology of sacrifice:

> ⁴Come to him, a living stone, though rejected by mortals yet chosen and precious in God's sight, and ⁵like living stones, let yourselves be built into a spiritual (*pneumatikos*) house, to be a holy priesthood, to offer spiritual sacrifices (*pneumatikas thusias*) acceptable to God through Jesus Christ.

Come to him uses the same verb that (in the Septuagint Greek translation of the Hebrew) describes the approach of the Jewish priest to the altar of sacrifice. *Living stone* refers obviously to Christ, and *living stones* obviously to Christians, thus recalling the *living sacrifice* of Rom. 12:1, and thus also combining in just two words Paul's earlier community-as-temple theme with his community/church images of building construction and plant growth. In its allusive richness the passage goes on to emphasize the importance of the proper internal dispositions for sacrifice, and the fact that true sacrifice means

---

Der Römerbrief (Freiburg/Vienna: Herder, 1977) 350-62, 430-31; Ulrich Wilckens, Der Brief an die Römer, vol. 3 (Zürich/Neukirchen-Vluyn: Neukirchener Verlag, 1982) 1-7, 118.

[47] See Daly, *Christian Sacrifice* (see p. viii, n. 1) 250-56; and *The Origins of the Christian Doctrine of Sacrifice* (also p. viii, n. 1) 65-67; also the major commentaries such as: Norbert Brox, *Der erste Petrusbrief* (Neukirchen-Vluyn: Neukirchener Verlag, 1979) 94-110; Reinhard Feldmaier, *Der erste Brief des Petrus*, Theologischer Handkommentar zum Neuen Testament 15/1 (Leipzig: Evangelische Verlagsanstalt, 2005) 88-94; Leonhard Goppelt, *Der erste Petrusbrief*, ed. Ferdinand Hahn (Göttingen: Vandenhoek & Ruprecht, 1978) 138-54; Ceslas Spicq, *Les Épîtres de Saint Pierre* (Paris: Librairie Lecoffre. J. Gabalda Cie, 1966) 79-84.

putting oneself totally, body and soul, at the disposition of God and neighbor. The *house* (i.e., temple) to be built of these *living stones* is *pneumatikos*/spiritual. This is the word that Christians increasingly favored over the *logikos* that Paul was still using in Rom. 12:1. It is the opposite of the idolatrous *cheiropoiētos*/made-with-hands we wrote about above (3.2.*b*. and *c*., pp. 72–73). This *house* is the temple in which true Christian sacrifices are to be offered and at the same time the dwelling place of God through Jesus Christ. Compactly emphasized are three vastly important themes: (1) the specifically Christian form of cultic spiritualization, (2) a theology of the divine acceptance of sacrifice, and (3) the mediatorship of Christ.

5 New Testament sacrifice is ethical

Before leaving the New Testament, it is important to note the remarkable convergence across the whole Testament on the nature and meaning of Christian sacrificial activity. But first, did the earliest followers of Jesus participate in the sacrificial rituals of the Jerusalem Temple? Paul's Nazirite sacrifice as narrated in Acts 21:23–26 obviously implies—they were, after all, observant Jews—that they did. Mt. 5:23–24 (see above at the end of 3.1.*b*., p. 73) implies the same. But by the time the gospels were being written five or more decades after the time of Jesus, it would seem that the early Christians, especially the early Gentile Christians, did not participate in ritual material sacrifice. Offering sacrifice, in the commonly understood sense of those words, was something that pagans did, and that Jews did, or used to do until the 70 AD destruction of the Temple, but not Christians. Nevertheless, biblical scholarship can identify five NT passages that, from their content and context, are obviously speaking specifically of Christian sacrificial activity. We find that, in each of these passages,[48] the activity involved is not ritual but ethical. In other words, supporting scientifically what Christian preachers have been proclaiming through the ages, modern critical exegesis finds that the primary idea of Christian sacrificial activity witnessed in the NT—and that includes the Epistle to the Hebrews, the most "sacrificial" of all the NT documents—is not liturgical or ritual but ethical and practical.

---

[48] Rom. 12:1–2; 15:15–16; 1 Pet. 2:4–10; Heb. 10:19–25; 12:18–13:16.

6 The Epistle to the Hebrews[49]

The unparalleled uniqueness of the Letter to the Hebrews cautions against making it, rather than the Letters of Paul, the basis for a Christian theology of sacrifice. But in any case there is nothing in Hebrews that cannot be complementarily harmonized with Paul. For in Hebrews as also in Paul, Christian life—indeed all Christian life, at least to the extent that it is authentically Christian—is ultimately spiritualized sacrifice. But it is important to emphasize how Paul's vision is broader than what can be strictly developed from Hebrews—for Paul sees apostolic missionary activity as priestly sacrificial ministry (Rom. 15:16). On the other hand, Hebrews shows more clearly the derivation of Christian sacrificial activity, spiritualized of course, from the once-for-all high-priestly sacrifice of Christ, referring, of course, to the culminating events of Jesus' earthly life. And this is what has captivated the imaginations of those Christian theologians who, even to this day, try to derive their idea of Christian sacrifice solely or primarily from the Epistle to the Hebrews.

3 Early Christianity

Preliminary note: The general situation

The early Christians, after overcoming those gnostic impulses and movements that either rejected the Old Testament or tried to distance themselves from it, saw themselves as the "New Temple," as members of the "New Covenant," and characterized their own holy writings as "*New* Testament." They also used sacrificial terminology to describe their foundational event, the death and resurrection of Christ and their own incorporation into that life with Christ. In doing this, they were appropriating the language and images of the pagan and Jewish sacrificial world around them,[50] as well as, in tension with that,

---

[49] See *Christian Sacrifice* (p. viii, n. 1); and *The Origins of the Christian Doctrine of Sacrifice* (also p. viii, n. 1). The most important critical commentaries are Harold W. Attridge, *The Epistle to the Hebrews* (Philadelphia, PA: Fortress Press, 1989); Otto Michel, *Der Brief an die Hebräer*, 6th ed. (Göttingen: Vandenhoeck & Ruprecht, 1966); and (for its extensive detail, though dated) Ceslas Spicq, *L'Epitre aux Hébreux*, 2 vols., 3rd ed. (Paris: Gabalda, vol 1, 1952; vol. 2, 1953).

[50] See Part 1.5, pp. 11–13, "The sacrificial world confronting ancient Christianity." The Romans tended to tolerate the non-sacrificing of the Jews in view of the antiquity of their traditions. The "newness"

the increasingly spiritualized theology of the Jewish sacrificial system. In that sacrificial world, when persecutions arose, at least external observance of pagan sacrificial practice served as a major practical criterion of distinction between Christians and pagans. For should any Christians offer sacrifice to the gods, they were breaking away from their faith and were no longer considered to be Christians, or at least, not Christians in good standing.[51] And when Christians, in loyalty to their faith did reject the sacrifices that the Roman state prescribed as a proof of loyalty to the gods of the state and to the emperor, they became targets of persecution. Sacrifice could thus be used as a "test" to identify and punish Christians.[52]

Now, at this point in our study, as we look beyond the New Testament to the earliest Christian documents, we find that Christianity's engagement with its ambient world was in its beginnings an engagement that was primarily with and within Judaism. But gradually, in the process of becoming that brand of "centrist Christianity" that, by the end of the fourth century, was winning the day, it had also become an engagement with non-Christian Antiquity. As we now look back to that time, we can see the early stages of the Christianity that, centuries later, along with Islam, had become one of the two dominant cultures of the Euro-Mediterranean world. But that begins the story of another still unresolved struggle.

a. *The Didache*[53]

The Didache, in genre a primitive church order, is considered by many to be the earliest of these non-biblical Christian documents. Although the document

---

of Christianity plus the Christians' insistence that they were not Jews generally prevented them from taking advantage of this "grandfathering" (presuming that they even wanted to).

[51] For example, Tertullian, *idol.* 1; *Conc. Elib. cn.* 1 [4, 241–42 Martinez Diéz/Rodriquez]. See the *RAC* articles "Apostasie" and "Exkommunikation"; also Christine Mühlenkamp, *Nicht wie die Heiden: Studien zur Grenze zwischen christliche Gemeinde und paganer Gesellschaft in vorkonstantinischer Zeit = Jahrbuch für Antike und Christentum* (Münster: Aschendorff, 2008) index, s.v. Opfer.

[52] Pliny, *ep.* 10.96; Lactantius, *inst.* 5, 11, 18; see the *RAC* articles: J. Vogt, "Christenverfolgung I," in *RAC* 2 (1954) 1159–1208; H. Last, "Christenverfolgung II," in *RAC* 2 (1954) 1208–28; K. Gross (E. Lieserung), "Decius," in *RAC* 3 (1957) 611–29; W. Seston, "Diocletianus," in *RAC* 3 (1957) 1036–53; regarding the Christians who offered sacrifice, Alfred Stuiber, "Lapsi," in *Lexikon für Theologie und Kirche*, 2nd ed. 6 (1961) 798; Pius Franchi de Cavalieri, *Scritti agiographici* 1–2 (Citta del Vaticano, 1962) 105–13 and index volume (ibid., 1964) 202 s.v. Sacrificii imposti ai cristiani.

[53] See Daly, *Christian Sacrifice* (p. viii, n. 1) 311–13; Aaron Milavec, *The Didache: Faith, Hope & Life of the Earliest Christian Communities, 50–70* C.E. (New York/Mahwah, NJ: Paulist Press, 2003);

as a whole probably dates from the late first to the early second century CE, the Eucharistic Prayers found in *Didache* 9 and 10 are much earlier. Most likely, because of their primitive Christology, they are even pre-gospel. For they are prayers addressed to "our Father," and within them Jesus is referred to not as Lord/*Kyrios*, but only as "your servant/*pais*." These prayers, which the author/redactor calls "eucharistizing" (*Did* 9.1 and 10.1) are probably what *Didache* 14 is referring to when it exhorts that confession of sins and fraternal reconciliation should precede the Sunday assembly "so that your sacrifice may be pure" (*Did* 14.2). Then, when the redactor changes Mal. 1:11 from a prophecy to a divine command: "In every place and time, offer to me a pure sacrifice" (*Did* 14.3),[54] it indicates that the author and his readers apparently already take for granted the idea of the Eucharist as sacrifice. But note that here in the *Didache*, apart from what Christians of a later age might project back into these texts, there is no suggestion, let alone any indication, that the death of Christ was seen as a sacrifice.

b. Clement of Rome[55]

Clement, bishop of Rome (ca. 96 CE), still in the trajectory of the increasingly spiritualizing Jewish tradition, emphasizes that true sacrifice is according to the will of God. He is concerned to institutionalize sacrifice, apparently meaning the Eucharist, within the life of the Church, and sees sacrifice as the characteristic function of the priestly office. But, as was also the case with the *Didache*, he does not make clear precisely what he means by "sacrifice." With nothing to suggest that Christians, except presumably for some Palestinian Jewish Christians before the 70 CE destruction of the temple, practiced material sacrifice, we have to assume that the meaning of sacrifice in such very early Christian texts is the spiritualized sacrifice of the prayer of praise and thanksgiving—as it was, for example, in Qumran (see Part 3.1.*f.*, pp. 68–69)— that for Christians also included, at least implicitly, the spiritualized offering— the Christian reinterpretation of sacrifice—of virtuous Christian living.

Huub van de Sandt, ed., *Matthew and the Didache: Two Documents from the Same Jewish-Christian Milieu?* (Assen: Royal van Gorcum/Minneapolis: Fortress Press, 2005).

[54] Mal. 1:11 reads: "For from the rising of the sun to its setting, my name is great among the nations, and in every place incense is offered to my name, and a pure offering."

[55] See Daly, *Christian Sacrifice* (p. viii, n. 1) 313–17.

c. Ignatius of Antioch[56]

With Ignatius of Antioch a decade later, there are two major developments. First the New-Testament temple theme is given a specifically Christian ecclesiological development by seeing the "one altar" or the state of being "within the altar" as symbols of church unity.[57] But second, and ominously, Christian ideas about sacrifice now find themselves at the center of Christianity's death struggle with non-Christian Antiquity. For, in contrast to the broad range of Christian living that Paul seemed to think of as sacrifice, it is much more narrowly his impending martyrdom in the Roman Colosseum that Ignatius has in mind as his sacrifice. Writing ahead to the Romans, his words, in their eucharistic sacrificial symbolism, are unforgettably, and for modern sensibilities almost grossly, graphic: "I am the wheat of God, and let me be ground by the teeth of the wild beasts that I may be found the pure bread of Christ . . . then shall I truly be a disciple of Christ, when the world shall see not so much as my body. Entreat Christ for me, that by these instruments I may be found a sacrifice (*thusia*) [to God]" (*Rom*. 4.1–2).

d. Justin Martyr and Athenagoras[58]

Some decades later the apologist, Justin (martyred ca. 167 CE), in conversation with both Judaism and pagan thinking, becomes the first Christian writer to treat sacrifice explicitly as a theological question. In condemning material sacrifice, he appropriates the Greek religious-philosophical critique of sacrifice, specifically the impropriety of offering material sacrifice to a spiritual God. But his condemnation of material sacrifice is not just philosophic, it is also specifically theological or religious. For he sees sacrifice as idolatry inspired by evil spirits. In this, and in his polemic in general, following the common polemical tactic of Antiquity's literate elites to attack the weaker positions of one's opponents, and in line with early Christianity's desire to separate itself from Judaism, he unfairly lumps Jewish sacrifice together with pagan sacrifice. But he also appropriates positively some aspects from the Jewish tradition, as

---

[56] Ibid., 318–21.
[57] *To the Ephesians* 5.2; *Philadelphians* 4; 7.2; *Trallians* 7.2; *Magnesians* 7.2.
[58] See Daly, *Christian Sacrifice* (p. viii, n. 1) 323–39.

can be seen in his theology of the divine acceptance of sacrifice, in his idea of Christ as the typological fulfillment of the Passover sacrifice, in his idea of Christ as sin offering, and in his idea of atonement as the purpose of sacrifice.[59] He shares with Ignatius the idea of the Eucharist as sacrifice, and even more explicitly than Ignatius, the idea that Christian sacrifice *is* the Eucharist (*Trypho* 4.13; 117.1–3). But unlike Ignatius, he does not narrowly identify this sacrifice with martyrdom. He writes:

> That prayers and giving thanks, when offered by worthy men, are the only perfect and pleasing sacrifices to God, I also admit. For such sacrifices are what Christians alone have undertaken to offer; and they do this in the remembrance effected by their solid and liquid food whereby the suffering endured by the Son of God is brought to mind. (*Trypho* 117.3)

Justin's fellow apologist and contemporary Athenagoras of Athens has roughly the same teaching. Athenagoras is also apparently the first to use what became a common phrase in reference to the Eucharist: "Bloodless sacrifice."[60]

e. Irenaeus of Lyons[61]

Irenaeus (ca. 130–ca. 200 CE) was born in Smyrna, though his work survives not in his original Greek but, for the most part, only in a possibly much later Latin translation. For him it was not the Jews, as it was with Justin, but rather the Gnostics who served as the major foil for his religious thought. He repeats the cult criticism of both the Hebrew prophets (*Adversus omnes Haereses* 4.26.1; 4.29.1–4) and the pagan philosophers and poets (3.12.11; 4.31.2). He does not view Old Testament Jewish sacrifice negatively, as Justin did, but as a providential preparation for Christian sacrifice (4.31.1). He sees Christ's physically real sacrifice as the very purpose of the Incarnation. And he sees communion between God and human beings and human sharing in divine

---

[59] *Apology* 1.37–39; *Dialogue with Trypho* 12.3; 15.4; 22.1; 28.5; 40.4; 41.1; 111.3–4; 112.1–2.
[60] Athenagoras, *Plea for the Christians* 13. This "apology," sometimes referred to as his "Supplication," was addressed by Athenagoras to the emperor Marcus Aurelius and his son Commodus around the year 177 CE. It can be found in all the standard collections of early Christian writing as, for example, in Vol. 2 of *The Ante-Nicene Fathers* (Grand Rapids, MI: Eerdmans, 1962 [reprint]) 129–48.
[61] See Daly, *Christian Sacrifice* (p. viii, n. 1 in Foreword) 339–60.

incorruptibility as the Incarnation's ultimate purpose.[62] His consciously anti-Gnostic pervasive sense of concrete physical realism is also reflected in his realistic understanding of eucharistic presence (see *Adv. Haer.* 4.31.3). Most of this is summed up in his extensive treatment of Christian sacrificial activity in *Adv. Haer.* 4.29.1–32, and especially concentrated in the following excerpt:

> But when he was instructing his disciples to offer to God the first-fruits of his creatures, not as if God needed this but that they themselves might be neither unfruitful nor ungrateful, he took that created thing, bread, and gave thanks, saying: "This is my body." And likewise the cup, which is part of that creation to which we belong, he confessed to be his blood, and taught the new oblation of the new covenant. This is what the church, receiving from the apostles, offers to God throughout the whole world, to him who gives for our subsistence the first fruits of his own gifts in the New Testament. This is what Malachi, one of the twelve prophets, thus foretold: "I have no pleasure in you, says the Lord almighty, and I will not accept sacrifice at your hands. For from the rising of the sun unto its setting my name is glorified among the nations and in every place incense is offered to my name, and a pure sacrifice; for my name is great among the nations, says the Lord Almighty" [Mal 1:10–12]. By this he indicates in the plainest manner that the former people shall indeed cease to make offerings to God, but that in every place sacrifice, indeed pure sacrifice—will be offered to him, and that his name will be glorified among the nations. (4.29.5)

Two further points: (1) What, precisely, does Irenaeus mean by "sacrifice," including especially his "oblation of the Church—*ecclesiae oblatio*" (*Adv. Haer.* 4.31.1)? As with those who went before him, Christian sacrifice, including eucharistic sacrifice, still seems to mean, primarily, lives lived in service and prayers offered in praise and thanksgiving. (2) Absent the original Greek, the traditional Latin translation of *Adversus omnes Haereses* seem to show, perhaps mistakenly, Irenaeus as holding a propitiatory (i.e., God-directed-human-action) idea of sacrificial atonement: Jesus "propitiating God for men—*propitians pro hominibus Deum*" (*Adv. Haer.* 4.16) or speaking of the true sacrifice "by offering which they shall appease God—*quod offerentes propitiabuntur Deum*" (4.29.2). However, these propitiatory ideas of sacrifice

---

[62] See *Proof of the Apostolic Preaching* 31.

may reflect more the assumptions of the later Latin translator—dates as late as 400 CE have been proposed for this translation—through whose pen this work has come down to us, than the actual thought and teaching of Irenaeus himself.[63]

f. Hippolytus of Rome[64]

The trajectory of meaning taking shape in our treatment of the early Christian writers—though we can neither assume nor claim that the later works were directly influenced by the earlier—continues in Hippolytus (ca. 170–ca. 236 CE). Less polemical than either the anti-Jewish Justin or the anti-Gnostic Irenaeus, he had, even more than Irenaeus, an intensely realistic, physical conception of the self-offering of the Word Incarnate. This connection between Incarnation and sacrifice became the leitmotif of his theology of sacrifice. He writes,

> I am not the one who says this, but he who has come down from heaven attests it; for he says: "No one has ascended into heaven but he who has descended from heaven, the Son of Man who is in heaven" (John 3:13). What then can he seek except what is proclaimed? Will he say that flesh was not in heaven? Yet there is the flesh that was presented by the Word of the Father as an offering, the flesh that came from the Spirit and the Virgin and was shown to be the perfect Son of God. It is evident, therefore, that he offered himself to the Father. (*Against Noetus* 4)[65]

This introduces a new "moment" in the development of the idea of Christian sacrifice: the eternal Word became human in order to rise again to heaven and there offer to the eternal Father not only his flesh, his own humanity, but also humanity itself. This offering to the Father enables Christians to share what the Father has granted to the Son, thus implying—but not yet explicitly spelling it out, as did the later Fathers—deification.[66]

---

[63] For the background of this substitutionary thinking, see Part 3.1.*d*., pp. 65–67.
[64] See Daly, *Christian Sacrifice* (p. viii, n. 1) 360–72.
[65] See also *The Refutation of All Heresies* 10.33.17.
[66] See Norman Russell, *The Doctrine of Deification in the Greek Patristic Tradition* (Oxford/New York: Oxford University Press, 2004); Stephen Finlan and Vladimir Kharlamov, *Theosis: Deification in Christian Theology* (Eugene, OR: Pickwick Publications, 2006 and Cambridge, England: James Clarke, 2010); Vladimir Kharlamov, ed., *Theosis. Volume 2: Deification in Christian Theology* (Eugene, OR: Pickwick Publications, 2011).

g. Passover treatises[67]

In the meantime, in the course of the second century, at least two Christian homiletic treatises on the Passover—the *Peri Pascha* (*PP, On the Passover*) of Melito of Sardis and the apparently Quartodeciman[68] *In S. Pascha* (*IP, On the Holy Passover*)—were giving a specifically Christian development to the Jewish Passover haggadah on Exodus 12. They expanded on the idea of the Eucharist and the Passion of Christ as the Christian Passover. For example: "This was the Pasch that Jesus desired to suffer for us [cf. Luke 22:15] by suffering he freed us from suffering, and by death he conquered death, and through the visible food he won for us his immortal life" (*IP* 49). But they were also developing a further theme, that of the spiritual Passover—*to logikon pascha*—giving a profoundly Christological meaning to the Greek words "*logos*" and "*logikos*." Half a century later, Origen's *Peri Pascha* (ca. 245) added a profoundly contemporary-existential meaning to this Christian Passover. He emphasized that what is of utmost importance—the "existential reality," to put it in modern terms—is the transformation, the "passing over" (*hyperbasis* or *diabasis*) in and with Christ that is now taking place in the lives of the Christians and on the altar of their souls. Origen wrote,

> We now raise the question whether it is only in that time of its concrete [i.e., historical] celebration that it (the sacred ceremony of the Passover) is carried out or whether we might not have to admit that it is also carried out in a different manner in our own time, the time of fulfillment—*upon whom the end of the ages has come*—1 Cor 10:11. (Origen, *PP* 39.16-23)

h. Martyrdom and sacrifice[69]

In these early centuries martyrdom is increasingly seen as the ultimate actualization of Christian sacrifice. When one sees Christ's death as sacrificial, as the early Christians were gradually beginning to do, and along with that

---

[67] See Daly, *Christian Sacrifice* (p. viii, n. 1) 373–78.
[68] The Quartodecimans, who survived as a sect into the fifth century, were those Christians who followed the Jewish practice of celebrating Easter/Passover on the actual fourteenth day of the month of Nisan rather than on the following Sunday.
[69] See Daly, *Christian Sacrifice* (p. viii, n. 1) 378–88, and Helgeland, Daly, and Burns, "The Military Martyrs," in *Christians and the Military* (see p. 18, n. 39 in Part 1) 55–66.

sees Christian life as an imitation of Christ, the explicit idea of martyrdom as sacrificial naturally follows. This is, in fact, richly witnessed in the second-century acts of the Christian martyrs. Although the language used by Christians to describe the courage and constancy of the martyrs in the face of their sufferings may at times sound like Stoicism, and may even show signs of Pelagianism and obvious hagiographical embellishment, one also finds in it a kind of Christ mysticism. The companions of the martyr Blandina "even with the eyes of the flesh saw in the person of their sister Him who was crucified for them" (*Letter of the Churches of Vienne and Lyons* 41). Felicitas, in the pains of childbirth, protests to those mocking her suffering: "Now I suffer what I suffer: but then another will be in me who will suffer for me, because I too am to suffer for him" (*Passion of SS. Perpetua and Felicitas* 15.3). Striking also is the concept of spiritual sacrifice that Apollonius, with proselytizing fervor, preaches to the judge who is about to condemn him:

> It was my hope, proconsul, that these religious discussions would help you and that the eyes of your soul would have been illumined by my defense, so that your heart would bear fruit and worship God the maker of all; and that to him alone, day by day and by means of almsgiving and brotherly love, you would offer your prayers, an unbloody and pure sacrifice to God. (*Acts of Apollonius* 44; see also 8)

i. Philo and the Christian Alexandrian tradition[70]

In the Christian Alexandrian tradition that (1) has roots at least as far back as the third-century BCE translation of the Hebrew Scriptures into the Greek Septuagint (LXX), and that (2) had its foundations broadly and deeply laid out by the Jewish religious philosopher Philo (ca. 20 BCE–ca. 50 CE), and that (3) finally reached its Christian maturity in Clement of Alexandria (ca. 150–ca. 215 CE) then Origen (ca. 185–ca. 254 CE), we find (4) that this Christian maturity involved Christian writers self-confidently appropriating their

---

[70] See Daly, *Christian Sacrifice* (p. viii, n. 1) 389–490; also Jean Daniélou, *Philon d'Alexandrie* (Paris: A. Fayard, 1958); Erwin Ramsdell Goodenough, *An Introduction to Philo Judaeus*, 2nd ed. (Oxford: Blackwell, 1962); Walter Völker, *Fortschritt und Vollendung bei Philo von Alexandrien: Eine Studie zur Geschichte der Frömmigkeit* (Leipzig: J. C. Hinrich, 1938); Harry Austryn Wolfson, *Philo: Foundations of Religious Philosophy in Judaism, Christianity, and Islam*, 2 vols. (Cambridge, MA: Harvard University Press, 1947).

Christian identity while also unself-consciously appropriating some of the religious-philosophical thinking of the ambient non-Christian literate elites. In other words, much of what later scholars would call the "natural theology" of someone like the Neoplatonist, Iamblichus[71] was hardly distinguishable from the natural theology of an Origen and of many of the more speculatively oriented Christian theologians of the later patristic golden age.

But the immediate story begins with Philo (see Part 2.4., pp. 32–33) whose overriding intent was to write an allegorical account of the human soul's progress toward God. From across his works one can cull out a highly developed theology of sacrifice that was surpassed in its richness only by the Christian Origen whose overall influence on Christian theology is, in turn, probably surpassed only by the Scriptures themselves. Combining Greek philosophy and Hebrew faith, Philo's favorite moral maxim on the subject of sacrifice—a maxim in principle also congenial to Greek philosophical thinking—also became foundational in the Christian idea of sacrifice: *We can only give to God what God has first given to us.*[72] Each of the following seven points summarizing his teaching on sacrifice (repeating what I reported above in 2.4.) became significant elements in the subsequent development of the Christian theology of sacrifice: (1) The Passover—which Philo saw as the life of virtue culminating in the mental turning toward education and wisdom—is a symbol of the soul's progress. (2) True sacrifice is an offering of the whole self: the soul, the mind, and the heart. (3) The divine acceptance of sacrifice and the primacy of dispositions are absolutely essential. (4) The purpose of sacrifice is, first, to honor God and, second, to benefit the worshiper. (5) His idea of the high priest, in his mind almost equated with the Logos, oscillates between Jewish idealization and Hellenistic spiritualization. (6) The idea of universal priesthood—conferred primarily by ethical purity—is central to his thinking on sacrifice. (7) His statements that had the most influence on Christian thinkers tended to center on the realities of temple, sanctuary, and altar. For example:

> There are, as is evident, two temples of God: one of them this universe, in which there is also as high priest his First-born, the divine Word, and the

---

[71] Ca. 250–ca. 330 CE; see 2.10, pp. 39–46.
[72] See: *On the Sacrifices of Cain and Abel* 97.

other the rational soul, whose priest is the real man; the outward and visible image of whom is he who offers the prayers and sacrifices handed down from our fathers.[73]

The true altar of God is the thankful soul of the Sage, compacted of perfect virtues unsevered and undivided, for no part of virtue is useless. On this soul-altar the sacred light is ever burning and carefully kept unextinguished, and the light of the mind is wisdom, just as the darkness of the soul is folly. (*On the Special Laws* 1.287)

Summing up, Philo's ideas of temple, soul, and altar stand in the service of his ethics, which, in turn is the mere propaedeutic of worship conceived in terms of its final goal, nonmaterial contemplation. Christians happily went along with his idea that worship essentially involves the ethical. But they did not absolutize Philo's contemplative goal. For Christian worship in this life is realized not so much—or at least not necessarily—in contemplation as in the living out of an incarnationally inspired life of service.

j. Barnabas[74]

The first Christian known to us to use a Philonic type of allegory, at least in the external structure of his thought, was the author of the *Epistle of Barnabas* from the second quarter of the second century. But somewhat like Justin, this writer is fiercely anti-Jewish in his view of OT sacrifices. And since he sees everything as pointing to Christ, his temple theology is much closer to the incarnational theology of Paul than to the radically spiritualizing theology of Philo (e.g., see *Barnabas* 16.6–10).

k. Clement of Alexandria[75]

Then, with Clement of Alexandria (ca. 150–ca. 215 CE) we come to what could be called a "Christian Philo." But what makes him clearly different from Philo as well as from his own gnostic contemporaries is his faith both in the Incarnation of Christ and in the Church as the mediator and guarantor

---

[73] *On Dreams* 1.215; cf. also *On Noah's Work as a Planter* 50 and *Who Is the Heir?* 75.
[74] See Daly, *Christian Sacrifice* (p. viii, n. 1) 422–40.
[75] Ibid., 440–87.

of the true, saving (i.e., Christian) gnosis. He tends to see things positively rather than in terms of a negative polemic. In his interpretation of Scripture, in which allegory is so dominant that the Bible seems more like a symbolic poem than as the object of exegesis, Clement uses the noun gnosis in both its adjectival and adverbial forms to refer to the true, spiritual meaning of Scripture. As in Philo, sacrifices are symbols of the soul's progress toward God. But in talking about them he also makes his own the cult criticism of the pagan intelligentsia in order to describe what the cult of the Christian, that is true gnosis, should be:

> The sacrifice acceptable to God is unswerving abstraction from the body and its passions. This is the really true piety. Is not, then, Socrates correct in calling philosophy the practice of death? . . . It was from Moses that the chief of the Greeks drew these philosophical tenets. For Moses commands holocausts to be skinned and divided into parts [cf. Lev. 1:6]. For the Gnostic soul must be consecrated to the light, stripped of the coverings of matter, separated from the frivolousness of the body and of all the passions which are acquired through vain and lying opinions, and divested of the lusts of the flesh. (*Stromata* 5.11)

Clement speaks of the sacrifice of Christ in a variety of ways: Christ as a whole burnt offering for us, Christ as the Passover, and Christ as the Suffering Servant and Lamb of God. He is also one of the earliest Christians to develop the Isaac-Christ typology.[76] Behind this, as already mentioned, is his belief in the Incarnation:

> For this also he came down. For this he clothed himself with man. . . . By bringing himself to the measure of our weakness whom he loved, he might correspondingly bring us to the measure of his own strength. And about to be offered up and giving himself as ransom, he left for us a new covenant-testament: "My love I give unto you." (*Quis dives salvetur* 37)[77]

Within this incarnational thinking the figure or image of Christ the high priest often provides the specific model for Clement's understanding of Christ's sacrifice. Here we find an interplay of three meanings of "high priest": the high

---

[76] See, for example, *Paedagogus* 1.5 and *Stromata* 2.5.
[77] See also *Stromata* 1.21; 5.6; *Paedagogus* 1.6.

priest of the Hebrew Scriptures, then Christ the high priest, and then—central to Clement's understanding of the Church and Christian sacrificial activity—the true Gnostic or Christian as high priest. Of this latter meaning Clement writes,

> Another way takes place when he [the Christian] who through him [Christ] has believed, takes off and puts on, as the apostle intimates, the consecrated stole [cf. Eph. 6:13–17]. Thence, after the image of the Lord, the worthiest were chosen from the sacred tribes to be high priests. (*Stromata* 5.6)

On this theme of Christian sacrificial activity, Clement faithfully develops the early Christian understanding of the relationship between the sacrifice of Christ and the sacrifice of—that is by—the Christian. He does this under three thematic headings: (1) the worship of the Gnostic, (2) universal priesthood, and (3) gnostic martyrdom. Of (1) *the worship of the Gnostic*, he writes: "Mildness, I think, and philanthropy, and eminent piety, are the rules of Gnostic Assimilation. I affirm that these virtues 'are a sacrifice acceptable in the sight of God'" (Phil. 4:18); for Scripture alleges that "the humble heart with right knowledge is the holocaust of God" (cf. Ps. 51:17, 19—LXX 50:19, 21) (*Stromata* 7.3). "We have become," he writes, "a consecrated offering to God for Christ's sake" (*Protrepticus* 4). This Christian worship is also strongly communal, a "sacrifice of the church":

> Breathing together is properly said of the church. For the sacrifice of the church is the word breathing as incense from holy souls, the sacrifice and the whole mind being at the same time unveiled to God . . . thus we should offer God not costly sacrifices but such as he loves. (*Stromata* 7.6)

Of (2) *universal priesthood* he writes that the true Gnostic is "the kingly man; he is the sacred high priest of God" (*Stromata* 4.25). While teaching this, he also takes care to point out, taking a position associated with the Donatists a few centuries later, that it is not by reason of ordination but by reason of virtue that the Gnostic is or becomes a presbyter (see *Stromata* 7.13). Of (3) *Gnostic Martyrdom*, seeing both blood martyrdom and gnostic martyrdom as sacrificial—as long as love towers over both—he writes,

> The Lord says in the gospel, "Whoever shall leave father or mother or brethren," etc. "for the sake of the gospel and my name" (Mt. 19:29), he is blessed; not indicating simple martyrdom, but the Gnostic martyrdom

[cf. also *Stromata* 4.14], as of the man who has conducted himself according to the rule of the gospel, in love to the Lord. (*Stromata* 4.4; cf. also 4.18)

On the theme of the temple and the altar, so strong in the Alexandrian tradition since Philo, Clement becomes the first Christian writer to see the reception of the Eucharist as enshrining Christ within the Christian(s) as in a temple:

> Such is the suitable food which the Lord ministers, and he offers his flesh and pours forth his blood, and nothing is wanting for the children's growth. O amazing mystery! . . . receiving him if we can, to hide him within and to enshrine the savior in our hearts so that we may correct the affections of our flesh. (*Paedagogus* 1.6)

In general, Clement moves smoothly from traditional spiritualizing temple criticism, to the Church as temple, to the Gnostic as temple, to the community as altar, and finally to both the individual soul and the assemblage of the elect as the altar from which rises the incense of holy prayer. In a passage that is typical but not unique, Clement writes,

> The altar, then, that is with us here, the terrestrial one, is the congregation of those who devote themselves to prayers, having as it were one common voice and one mind. . . . Now breathing together is properly said of the church. For the sacrifice of the church is the word breathing as incense from holy souls, the sacrifice and the whole mind being at the same time unveiled to God. (*Stromata* 7.6)

l. Minucius Felix

In *Octavius*, a fictitious dialogue between Octavius, an educated Christian and Caecilius, an educated pagan, Minucius Felix, a late-second/early-third-century Christian apologist—apparently an African writing in Latin—contrasts the unbloody sacrifices of the Christians with the bloody sacrifices of the pagans. In this dialogue his Christian character, Octavius, proudly proclaims that the sacrifices that please God are a good heart, a pure mind, and undefiled thoughts. Thus, those who are standing guard over their innocence are offering prayer to God. Octavius continues in a vein that, while using the graphically literal language of bloody animal sacrifice, thoroughly appropriates a spiritualized understanding of it:

the one who practices justice is offering sacrifice to God (*deo libat*). They who refrain from dishonesty are finding favor with God. And whoever rescues someone from danger is offering God the most beautiful sacrifice of all (*optimam victimam caedit*).[78] These are our sacrifices (*nostra sacrificia*), and this is our worship (*dei sacra*); for it is the rectitude of a person that counts for us as the measure of one's piety. (*Octavius* 32.2–3)[79]

m. Tertullian[80]

Tertullian (ca. 160–ca. 225), often called the Father of Latin Theology, emphasizes against both Jews and pagans, and usually in an aggressively apologetic and polemical tone, that Christians do not offer material sacrifice, but only spiritual sacrifice. Building on Mal. 1:10–11, a favorite text from the Hebrew Bible that the early Christians liked to change from prophecy into Christian fulfillment,[81] Malachi's "pure offering" becomes what Christians celebrate when they "assemble to read [their] sacred writings" (*Apology* 39.5). And what the Christians actually offer when they so gather is not just their prayers but their very selves, along with their good works:

> This victim, devoted from the whole heart, fed on faith, tended by truth, entire in innocence, pure in chastity, garlanded with love, we ought to escort with the pomp of good works, amid psalms and hymns, unto God's altar, to obtain for us all things from God. (*De oratione* 28)

Without explicitly referring to Rom. 12:1—"offer your *bodies* as a spiritual sacrifice"—Tertullian seems to be expanding on the meaning of that seminal sacrificial text. For he takes pains to emphasize that "*it is the flesh* . . . *that*

---

[78] "Most beautiful sacrifice of all" is a weak translation of the metaphor in *optimam victimam caedit* which literally, means the much more graphically bloody: "slaughters a/the most perfect victim."
[79] *The Octavius of Marcus Minucius Felix*, translated and annotated by Graeme Wilber Clarke (New York: Newman Press, 1978); see also Jean de Watteville, *Le sacrifice dans les textes eucharistiques des premières siècles* (Neuchâtel/Paris: Delachaux et Niestlé, 1966) 128.
[80] This section and the following section are a translation/modified adaptation of what was originally written by Theresa Dockter (née Nesselrath) in the *RAC* 26.183–84 (p. viii, see n. 1 and n. 2).
[81] "Oh, that someone among you would shut the temple doors, so that you would not kindle fire on my altar in vain! I have no pleasure in you, says the Lord of hosts, and I will not accept an offering from your hands. For from the rising of the sun to its setting my name is great among the nations, and in every place incense is offered to my name, and a pure offering; for my name is great among the nations, says the Lord of hosts" (Mal. 1:10–11).

performs those sacrifices" (De resurrectione 8.4); and "that costly and noble sacrifice of prayer *despatched from the chaste body*" (*Apology* 30.5).

This pure sacrifice that Christians offer: *gloriae scilicet relatio et benedictio et laus et hymnus*,[82] are the actions of a truly incarnational spiritualization, for along with prayer Tertullian lists fasting and virginity among the spiritual sacrifices that come from contrition of the heart and true love of God and that make the Christians themselves holy and into a sacrificial offering that glorifies God.[83] And finally, summing up and expressing much of this meaning, Tertullian also speaks of the Eucharist as sacrifice: *sacrificium*[84] or *oblatio*.[85] Nowhere, however, does he, as Justin had begun to do, give any description of the Eucharistic "action."[86] By now, at least Tertullian's Christians apparently no longer had difficulty, as did earlier Christians, in thinking of the crucifixion death of Christ as a sacrifice.

n. Cyprian

A bit later in the Latin West, Cyprian of Carthage (d. 258 CE), the first one to connect the Eucharist in a special way with Christian priests, understands the sacrifice of Christ as the *object* of the eucharistic offering. In other words, presaging a view that later became common in the Christian West, and then fiercely challenged by the Protestant reformers, the Eucharist is beginning to be seen as a sacrifice offered by Christian priests. It is an imitation of and the sacrament of the sacrifice of the Lord *sacrificii Domini sacramentum*,[87]

---

[82] *Adv. Marc.* 3.22.6; cf. *Adv. Iud.* 5.4–7; Karl Suso Frank, "Maleachi 1, 10ff in der frühen Väterdeutung. Ein Beitrag zu Opferterminologie und Opferverständnis in der alten Kirche," *Theologie und Philosophie* 53 (1978) 76.

[83] *ieiun.* 7.16; *res.* 8.4; *apol.* 30.5f; Everett Ferguson, "Spiritual Sacrifice in Early Christianity and Its Environment," *ANRW* 2.23.2 (1980) 1184f; Franz Ser. Renz, *Opfercharakter der Eucharistie nach der Lehre der Väter und Kirchenschriftsteller der ersten drei Jahrhunderten* (1892); de Watteville, *Le sacrifice dans les textes eucharistiques des premières siècles* (see p. 93, n. 79 in Part 3) 118.

[84] *orat.* 19, 1. 4; *cult. fem.* 2, 11, 2.

[85] *Cor.* 3.3; Johannes Betz, *Eucharistie in der Schrift und Patristik*. Handbuch der Dogmengeschichte 4a (Freiburg: Herder, 1979) 144.

[86] See Victor Saxer, "Tertullian," in Willy Rordorf and Others, *The Eucharist of the Early Christians* (New York: Pueblo Publishing Company, 1978) 132–55 [= ET of *L'Eucharistie des Premiers Chrétiens* (Paris: Beauchesne et ses Fils, 1976)].

[87] *ep.* 63.4.1; Ferguson, "Spiritual Sacrifice in Early Christianity and Its Environment" (see above, n. 83) 1185; de Watteville, *Le sacrifice dans les textes eucharistiques des premières siècles* (see above, n. 79) 145; cf. Clemens Leonard and Benedikt Eckhardt, "Mahl V" (Kultmahl) above in *RAC* vol. 23, 1084f., 1096f; Herbert Schmid, "Eucharistie und Opfer. Das 'Evangelium des Judas' im Kontext von Eucharistiedeutungen des 2. Jahrhunderts," *Early Christianity* 3, no. 1 (2012) 85–108, at 86; extensive

the sacrifice that Jesus celebrated; and it is itself the very sacrifice in which Jesus himself is both the priest and offering: "We make mention of the Passion in all sacrifices that we offer (for the Lord's passion is the sacrifice which we offer.)"[88] Since Cyprian also understands the subjective imitation of the obedient suffering of Jesus as sacrifice, he can give encouragement to all those who are banished in persecution or condemned to forced labor, and not able to participate in the sacrifices offered by the priests, for your "broken spirit ... broken and contrite heart" are also precious and magnificent sacrifices that you are day and night offering to God.[89]

o. Origen of Alexandria[90]

Meanwhile, in the Greek-speaking Alexandrian tradition, we have the towering theological figure of Origen (ca. 185–ca. 254 CE), the great theologian of sacrifice, as Harnack called him.[91] For the most part, practically all that was in Clement of Alexandria (see Part 3.3.*k*., pp. 89–92) we find developed even further here. But one significant difference, as we have already seen in his *Peri Pascha*, is that Origen's primary referent, his primary hermeneutical key, is not what happened in the past, whether at the first Passover in Egypt or even in its fulfillment in Christ's sacrificial death, but what is happening right now in the here-and-now life of the Christian who is still in the process of "passing over" in and with Christ (see Part 3.3.*g*., p. 86). Origen speaks of Christ's sacrifice in the many ways that Clement did, but beyond that, he emphasizes, in a way that we have just seen Cyprian beginning to do, and that Augustine and later Christians also enthusiastically did, namely, that Christ is both priest and victim in his unique offering to the Father. As powerful as was Clement's use of the temple theme as an aid to seeing the whole of Christian life as an

---

treatment of Cyprian's Eucharistic teaching in Bernard Renaud, "Eucharistie et culte eucharistique selon saint Cyprien," diss. Louvain (1967).

[88] *ep.* 63.17.1; Betz, *Eucharistie in der Schrift und Patristik* (see p. 94, n. 85) 145; Renz, *Opfercharakter der Eucharistie* (see p. 94, n. 83) 145.

[89] *ep.* 76.3 with quotation from Ps. 51 [50]:19; de Watteville, *Le sacrifice dans les textes eucharistiques des premières siècles* (see p. 93, n. 79) 145f.

[90] See Robert J. Daly, "Sacrifice in Origen," *Studia Patristica* 11; Texte und Untersuchungen 108 (Berlin: Akademie Verlag, 1972) 125–29; idem, *The Origins of the Christian Doctrine of Sacrifice* (p. viii, see n. 1) 122–27.

[91] Adolf von Harnack, *Lehrbuch der Dogmengeschichte*, 4th ed., 2 vols. (Tübingen: J.C.B. Mohr, 1909–10) 1.477.

incarnated participation in Christ's sacrifice, this gets developed even more powerfully in Origen, especially in his use of the "living stones" image from 1 Pet. 2:5. Summing up and combining numerous passages from Origen, we could say that

> [Origen] exhorts us to refuse to build merely lifeless temples; for our body is a temple of God, and the best of these temples is the body of Jesus Christ. The temple that has been destroyed will be rebuilt of living and most precious stones, with each of us becoming a precious stone in the great temple of God. As living stones we must also be active. For if, says Origen, I raise my hands in prayer, but leave hanging the hands of my soul instead of raising them with good and holy works, then the raising of my hands is not an evening sacrifice.[92]

For Origen, much more than for Clement whose emphasis was on gnostic martyrdom, actual martyrdom was the privileged way for Christians to share in the sacrifice of Christ. Then, recalling that the book of Revelation sees the martyrs standing next to the heavenly altar of sacrifice, Origen is able to see and teach that Christian sacrifice, while acted out in this world, has its fulfillment only eschatologically, that is, in the eternal now of heaven. We will return to this theme later in our treatment of sacrifice in the development of the Eucharistic anaphora (see 3.3.*t*., pp. 107–10).

p. From Origen to Augustine

In this section we will briefly sketch the development between the two important "poles" of Origen in the East and Augustine in the West. Having just spoken of the "towering figure of Origen," we are now looking ahead to Augustine (see below 3.3.*q*. and *r*., pp. 100–2), the second of the two, so to speak, "twin towers" of early Christian theology. Should one, as a thought experiment, take away Origen and his influence, the subsequent development of Christian theology would become difficult to explain. A similar claim could be made regarding Augustine: take away Augustine and his influence, the subsequent development of Western (i.e., Latin) Christian theology becomes

---

[92] See especially *Against Celsus* 8.19; *Dialogue with Heraclides* 20; *Homilies on Numbers* 20.3—quoted from Daly, *Sacrifice Unveiled* (see p. viii, n. 1) 94.

similarly difficult to explain. This offers some justification for the small attention we give in this book on sacrifice to the otherwise important eight theological figures we treat briefly in the following section. By this date, as our readers will have noticed, when early Christian authors are talking about Christian sacrifice, they are usually also talking about the Eucharist. See "Excursus 4: The Eucharist as sacrifice" (114–20).

aa. From Lactantius to Ephrem the Syrian[93]

The early Latin apologist Lactantius (ca. 250–ca. 325) insisted that, because God is the Word, God ought to be sacrificed to in words, and thus not with bloody animal offerings but with the spiritual offerings of a good heart, good deeds, hymns of praise, or, as he put it in terms pregnantly reminiscent of Rom. 12:1, in a sacrifice *hominis et vitae*, literally, "of man and of life."[94]

Eusebius of Caesarea (ca. 260–ca. 340) sees prayer,[95] and especially the prayer of the Eucharist, as sacrifice:

> We offer sacrifice and incense in that we carry out the remembrance of his great sacrifice according to the mysteries he has given us, and offer God the salvation-bringing Eucharist through pious hymns and prayers, and also by the fact that we sanctify ourselves wholly for him and dedicate ourselves with body and soul to his High Priest the great Logos.[96]

Much of Eusebius's teaching on sacrifice is connected with his overly enthusiastic program of adulation for the emperor Constantine, seeing him as offering the souls of the flock entrusted to him which he leads to the pious veneration of God. Eusebius even goes so far as to describe the 325 CE Council of Nicea as Constantine's thank-offering for his victory. But there is also real

---

[93] This section is a translation/modified adaptation of what was originally written by Theresa Dockter (née Nesselrath) in the *RAC* 26.185–89 (see p. viii, n. 1 and n. 2).

[94] *Divinae Institutiones* 6.1.24–25; 6.25.12; Ferguson, "Spiritual Sacrifice in Early Christianity and Its Environment" (see p. 94, n. 83) 1184, 1186; de Watteville, *Le sacrifice dans les textes eucharistiques des premières siècles* (see p. 93, n. 79 in Part 3) 151.

[95] *Vita Constantini* 1.48; 4.45. On the unbloody sacrifice of thanksgiving in the commemoration of the martyrs, see the sermon *Ad coetum sanctorum* 12 (*GCS* Eusebius 1.171); *Demonstratio evangelica* 1.10.36–38; Ferguson, "Spiritual Sacrifice in Early Christianity and Its Environment" (see p. 94, n. 83) 1188–89.

[96] *Demonstratio evangelica* 1.10.38 (translation adapted from Betz, *Eucharistie in der Schrift und Patristik* [see p. 94, n. 85]) 68. See also *Historia ecclesiastica* 10.4.68: Christ is the High Priest who stands at the altar of the Church and accepts the unbloody, immaterial sacrifice offered in prayer.

theology in Eusebius. He sees the Eucharist as the spiritual (*logikē*) sacrifice in which Christ gives himself as food, a sacrificial memorial and memorial sacrifice, already foreshadowed in the sacrifices of the patriarchs.[97]

Next we come to the three great Cappadocian Fathers: Basil the Great (ca. 330–79), Gregory of Nazianzus (ca. 330–ca. 390), and Gregory of Nyssa (ca. 330–ca. 395). In Basil, the first to mention the role of the Holy Spirit in the development of the specifically Christian idea of sacrifice,[98] the spiritual sacrifice of praise and thanksgiving is carried out only in and with the help of the Holy Spirit. For Gregory of Nazianzus, the most prolific of the Cappadocians on sacrifice, as well as the most devotionally inclined and literarily gifted, the unbloody (see Athenagoras Part 3.3.*d.*, p. 83) sacramental eucharistic sacrifice[99] signifies a divinizing "communion with Christ himself, with his Passion and his Divinity."[100] When the spiritual sacrifices of fasting, almsgiving, and good works get practiced, they reconcile the anger of God that would be flaring up because of the lack of such virtues.[101] For ultimately, as Rom. 12:1 teaches, (bodily) human beings are the single worthy gift that can be offered to God.[102] Gregory of Nyssa also sees the Eucharist as a kind of sacrifice of atonement. With Jesus as High Priest offering himself for our sins,[103] priests especially must be measured against that example:

> Whoever wishes to be a priest must also bring his body in sacrifice and himself become a sacrificial victim, not a dead sacrifice, in his living and spiritual service; he should not become a burden to souls by a comfortable and all too fleshly style of life, but rather, he should by his pure life wipe away like a cobweb all the necessities of life.[104]

---

[97] *Laus Constantini* 2–3; *Vita Constantini* 3.7.2; 15.1; *Demonstratio evangelica* 1.10.1–19 and 29; *Commentary on the Psalms* 15.3; Betz, *Eucharistie in der Schrift und Patristik* (see p. 94, n. 85) 88; Frances Young, "Opfer. IV. NT und Alte Kirche," *TRE* 25 (1995) 271–78, at 275.
[98] *On the Holy Spirit* 26.62–63 (*Sources Chrétiennes* 17bis, 473–74).
[99] *ep.* 171 (*GCS* 53, 123); cf. Young, "Opfer" (see above, n. 97) 276.
[100] *Oration* 4.52 (*Sources Chrétiennes* 309.156); Betz, *Eucharistie in der Schrift und Patristik* (see p. 94, n. 85) 70; *Carmina poemata* 1.2.34, 238f (*PG* 37.962–63).
[101] *Oration* 16.6.13 (*PG* 35.941–44. 952); Frances M. Young, *The Use of Sacrificial Ideas in Greek Christian Writers from the New Testament to John Chrysostom* (Cambridge, MA: Philadelphia Patristic Foundation, 1979) 231–32.
[102] *Oration* 42.8 (*Sources Chrétiennes* 384.68–70); Young, "Opfer" (see above, n. 97) 274.
[103] *c. Eunom.* 3.4.19 (*GregNyssOp* 2.140–41); Betz, *Eucharistie in der Schrift und Patristik* (see p. 94, n. 85) 70; Johannes Maier, *Die Eucharistielehre der drei großen Kappadozier, des hl. Basilius, Gregor von Nazianz und Gregor von Nyssa* (Freiburg im Breisgau: Herder, 1915) 38.
[104] *vit. Moys.* 2 (*GregNyssOp* 7.1.98–99); *virg.* 23 (ibid., 8.1.342–43); Maier, *Die Eucharistielehre der drei großen Kappadozier* (see above, n. 103) 33–34.

The death of the protomartyr Stephen is seen as an imitation of the sacrifice of Christ: "As a priest he offered up his own body in sacrifice; his prayer washed away the sins of murderers and brought about forgiveness."[105]

The understanding of Christian sacrifice and the eucharistic sacrifice found in the Cappadocians is solidified in John Chrysostom (ca. 347–407). In all the various Eucharistic celebrations, the sacrificial gift and the sacrificial giver is the same, Jesus Christ.[106] This is because of the mystical identity of the Last Supper with both Christ and the currently celebrating priest. In Chrysostom's words, as interpreted for us by Johannes Betz: "The sacrifice is the same, whether this one or that one, whether Paul or Peter offers it. It is the same that Christ once gave to his disciples and that now the priests carry out."[107] In words pregnant with the way that worshippers to this day can experience the Divine Liturgy: "We enjoy the same Body that thrones on high."[108]

Aphrahat, an early-fourth-century ascetic monk, the first of the Syriac Church Fathers, taught that the sacrifices of the Old Testament had been rejected and replaced by Christian prayer. And, in his mind, the perfection of prayer involved ministry to one's neighbor.[109]

Ephrem the Syrian (ca. 306–73), founder of the Syrian school, exegete, apologist, preacher, ascetical writer, and, above all, brilliant writer of hymns, saw the Eucharist as a realistic re-presentation of Christ's self-offering. It was a remarkable patristic presaging of the ecumenically fertile early-twentieth-century—Dom Odo Casel—theology of *Vergegenwärtigung*: a profoundly real and not just symbolic interpenetration of the sacrifice of Christ and the sacrifice of Christians. Ephrem saw Christ as giving his unique self-sacrifice

---

[105] Young, "Opfer" (see p. 98, n. 97 in Part 3) 273.
[106] *In Mt. hom.* 25.3; 50.3 (*PG* 57.331; 58.508); *in Hebr. hom.* 17,3 (ibid., 63.131); Betz, *Eucharistie in der Schrift und Patristik* (see n. 85 in Part 3) 73–74, 101–4.
[107] *In 2 Tim. Hom.* 2.4 (*PG* 62.612; transl. from Betz, *Eucharistie in der Schrift und Patristik* [see p. 94, n. 85]).
[108] *In Eph. Hom.* 3.3 (ibid., 62.27); cf. in *Hebr. hom.* 14.1 (ibid., 63.111). For an extensive treatment of the sacrificial character of the Eucharist according to John Chrysostom, cf. for example August Naegle, *Die Eucharistielehre des heiligen Johannes Chrysostom, des Doctor Eucharistiae* (Freiburg im Breisgau: Herder, 1900) 148–231.
[109] Aphrahat, *Demonstrations* 4.13–14 and 18–19 (*Patrologia Syriaca* 1.1165–72 and 176–81). See Dimitry F. Bumazhnov, "Gebet als Opfer in Dem IV des Aphrahat," in Hans Klein, Vasile Mihoc, and Karl-W. Niebuhr, eds., *Das Gebet im Neuen Testament* (Tübingen: Mohr Siebeck, 2009) 434.

into the hands of Christians. In offering it, Christians are themselves offered and made holy.[110]

q. Augustine

With Augustine of Hippo (354–430) we have moved ahead some 170 years from the pre-Nicene Greek-speaking Christianity of Alexandria to the post-Nicene, Constantinopolitan, and now Latin-speaking Christianity of North Africa. In Book 10 of the *City of God*, Augustine offers the beginning of a systematic treatment of sacrifice. He notes, as did Aristotle at the beginning of his *Nichomachean Ethics*, the universal human desire for happiness/blessedness. He then recalls the by-now traditional philosophical critique of sacrifice (God doesn't need it; it is for our benefit, not God's, etc.), before moving on to express his Christian, and at least implicitly trinitarian, sense of the ultimate identity between the "law" of sacrifice and the "law" of love. He then sums up much of this in a definition:

> *Proinde verum sacrificium est omne opus, quo agitur, ut sancta societate inhaereamus Deo, relatum scilicet ad illum finen boni, quo veraciter beati esse possimus* [Thus, true sacrifice is every work which is done in order that we might be one with God in a holy society, i.e., a work which is related to that end of the good by which we can be truly happy]. (*City of God* 10.6)

r. Origen and Augustine compared[111]

The normative influence of Origen on later Christian thinking, and not just in the Greek East, is significantly paralleled by Augustine's influence on the later Latin West. The theology of sacrifice of these two authoritative Christian thinkers is, in substance, remarkably similar, but with some—ultimately quite revelatory—differences. For one thing, Augustine's "definition" is very different from what Origen would have written. It sounds more like the somewhat

---

[110] Ephrem, *Hymn* 31.5 (*Corpus scriptorum Christianorum orientalium* 224-*Scriptores Syri* 95.98); cf. *Hymn. de azymis* 2.7 (ibid., 249-Syr. 109.4); *Hymn de crucifix.* 3.10 (ibid., 41); *Sermo de domino nostro* 50 (CSCO 271-*Scriptores Syri* 117.48; see Betz, *Eucharistie in der Schrift und Patristik* (p. 94, n. 85) 71–72.
[111] See Robert J. Daly, "Sacrifice in Origen and Augustine: Comparisons and Contrasts," *Studia Patristica* 19 (1989) 148–53.

Aristotelian scholasticism yet to come than the Platonism that Augustine had in common with Origen. Then, when we contrast Augustine with Origen using the threefold scheme of sacrifice of Christ, temple themes, sacrifice by Christians, the differences become especially revelatory.

First, under the *sacrifice of Christ,* while Origen sees Christ's sacrificial redemptive work as being completed only when Christ returned to the Father in heaven, focusing, in a somewhat Platonizing way, more on the heavenly realities of which the sacrifices here below are but a "copy and shadow" (Heb. 8:5), Augustine, in contrast, tends to see Christ's sacrificial redemptive activity as having been completed *in this world*. This is analogous to the difference between the Neoplatonist Iamblichus seeing personal sanctification, and the Roman Symmachus seeing the empire-supporting *pax deorum*, as the end and purpose of sacrifice (see Part 2.10. and 2.12., pp. 39–46 and 49–50).

Second, under *temple themes* there is another significant difference. Origen, though committedly incarnational, remains quite at home with the Philonic and Platonic ideas of the ascent of the soul (*psychē*) or mind (*nous*). By contrast, and despite his high regard for Platonic philosophy, Augustine seems to be attempting to distance himself from Platonic categories by the way in which he views the internal altar less as the soul or mind and more as the bodily human heart.

Third, under *sacrifice by Christians,* using practically the same words as Origen, Augustine also teaches, the theology of Christ as both the priest and victim in his sacrifice, and of Christians themselves as the sacrifice that they, too, when united with Christ, offer to God. But here too there is a huge difference: again analogous to the Iamblichus/Symmachus contrast, what is most significant for Origen is that which is taking place before the heavenly throne of God, while, in contrast, Augustine's concept of the city of God has him attributing much more importance to what is taking place here in this world. The "holy society/*sancta societas*" of Augustine's definition emphatically emphasizes the members of the Church here on earth along with the blessed in heaven. This emphasis comes out loud and clear in his words:

> This he [Christ] offered, in this he was offered, because it is in this way that he is the mediator; in this he is the priest, in this he is the sacrifice . . . [and] we ourselves are this whole sacrifice . . . this is the sacrifice of Christians: that we, though we are many, are one body in Christ. The Church celebrates

this mystery in the sacrament of the altar, as the faithful know, and there she shows them clearly that in what is offered, she herself is offered. (*City of God* 10.6)

Very significant, especially for later developments is the way in which Augustine—and, of course, he is anything but alone in doing so—seems to identify this "sacrifice of Christians" with the Eucharist. For example, a bit later he writes, "To eat the bread, which in the New Testament is the sacrifice of Christians [*manducare panem, quod est in novo testamento sacrificium Christianorum*]" (*City of God* 17.5). To sum up, we have highlighted how

> Augustine, in a way that became more or less normative for most of the Christianity in the West, made a strong point of including earthly as well as heavenly members as citizens in God's city, and who, precisely in their role as being here-and-now earthly members of Christ's body, become one with him in being both the priests and the victims, those who offer and who are offered in the liturgy that is their Christian lives.[112]

And finally, one must also keep in mind how ambiguously, and sometimes even confusedly, both Platonic and incarnationally "trans-Platonic" is so much of the Christian tradition from Clement of Alexandria and Origen onward. For example, Augustine, not surprisingly due to his belief in the Incarnation, and despite his Neoplatonist tendencies, insisted that the altar on which Christians offer true sacrifice is the altar of the heart. But that very phrase, as Toulouse points out in his magisterial study of Neoplatonist sacrifice,[113] possibly comes from the radically spiritualizing, anti-Christian Neoplatonist Porphyry (see Parts 2.9. and 10., pp. 38–46).

s. The cult of the martyrs and the Eucharist

At this point we will round off our summary of early Christian ideas on sacrifice by pointing out how they also took shape in connection with the cult of the martyrs and the early development of the eucharistic anaphora.

---

[112] Quoted from Daly, *Sacrifice Unveiled* (see pp. viii, n. 1) 97.
[113] Stéphane Toulouse, "Que le vrai sacrifice es celui d'un coeur pur: À propos d'un oracle 'porphyrien' (?) dans le Liber xxi sententiarum édité parmi les oeuvres d'Augustin," *Recherches Augustiniennes* 32 (2001) 169–223, at 207.

Some aspects of this particular trajectory go back at least to the pre-Christian Maccabean martyrs. After that, the at least implicitly martyrological ways in which the New Testament talks about the sacrifice of Christ and his Last Supper add significant impetus to this trajectory that, then, in the apostolic age becomes powerfully explicit in the unforgettably graphic terms, both obviously eucharistic and explicitly sacrificial, with which Ignatius of Antioch (see 3.3.c., p. 82) speaks of his impending martyrdom: "I am the wheat of God, and let me be ground by the teeth of the wild beasts that I may be found the pure bread of Christ... then shall I truly be a disciple of Christ, when the world shall see not so much as my body. Entreat Christ for me, that by these instruments I may be found a sacrifice [to God]" (Ignatius, To the Romans 4.1–2).

One would expect such words to have found enthusiastic resonance among those early Christians who also had to face the threat of martyrdom. There are indeed some obvious echoes in the Christ mysticism of the early Christian Acts of the Martyrs, but for clear evidence of an explicit development of the martyr-sacrifice-Eucharist connection we have to wait until *The Martyrdom of Polycarp*. This document is ostensibly a letter from the church at Smyrna to the other Christian churches giving an account of Polycarp's death. Although it is traditionally dated to February 23, 155/6 CE, recent scholarship dates this document not from the time immediately following Polycarp's martyrdom, but from the middle of the third century, one hundred years later.[114] In other words, this document, recognized as the foundational document or star witness for the early Christian cult of the martyrs, comes from approximately the time of the persecution of Decius (d. 251 CE) who, in 249, had commanded all subjects to sacrifice and obtain certificates of their obedience, thus setting off the first empire-wide persecution of the Christians.

Since this document, *The Martyrdom of Polycarp*, our earliest literary evidence and indeed star witness for the existence of the cult of the martyrs, reflects the more advanced theological nuance of the next century, assigning its date not to the actual time of Polycarp but to the middle of the third

---

[114] See Candida Moss, *The Other Christs: Imitating Jesus in Ancient Christian Ideologies of Martyrdom* (New York/London: Oxford University Press, 2010).

century enables the critical historian to read it as etiological—a (usually later) explanation of the cause or origin of something—rather than as prophetic. The following words thus make more sense as the account of an already established memorial celebration, rather than of one just beginning:

> And thus it came about that we afterwards took up his bones, more precious than costly stones and more excellent than gold, and interred them in a decent place. There the Lord will permit us, as far as possible, to assemble in rapturous joy and celebrate his martyrdom—his birthday—both in order to commemorate the heroes that have gone before, and to train and prepare the heroes yet to come.[115]

The same approach, reading it as etiology rather than prophecy, enables us to be comfortable in dating to the mid-third-century Polycarp's final prayer that the narrator introduces with the words: "And there he was, with his hands put behind him, and fastened, like a ram towering above a large flock, ready for sacrifice, a holocaust prepared and acceptable to God! And he looked up to heaven and said . . ." (*Martyrdom* 14, p. 97). Polycarp's prayer which then follows has, as has often been noted, the basic structure of an eucharistic anaphora in three parts: **A.** anamnesis, that is, praise and thanksgiving; **B.** epiclesis, that is, supplication or petition; and **C.** final doxology. For clarity, I insert the **A. B. C.** designations within the citation:

> **A.** O Lord God, O Almighty, Father of Thy beloved and blessed Son Jesus Christ, through whom we have received the knowledge of you—*God of angels and hosts of all creation*—and of the whole race of saints who live under your eyes! I bless Thee, because Thou hast seen fit to bestow upon me this day and this hour, that I may share, among the number of the martyrs, the cup of Thy Anointed and *rise to* eternal *life* both in soul and in body in virtue of the immortality of the Holy Spirit. **B.** May I be accepted among them in Thy sight today as a rich and pleasing sacrifice, such as Thou, the true God that cannot utter a falsehood, hast prearranged, revealed in advance, and now consummated. **C.** And therefore I praise Thee for everything; I bless Thee; I glorify Thee through the eternal and heavenly High Priest Jesus Christ, Thy beloved Son, through whom be glory to Thee together with Him and

---

[115] *Martyrdom of Polycarp* 18.2–3 (trans. James H. Kleist, *Ancient Christian Writers* 6 [1948] 99).

the Holy Spirit, both now and for the ages to come. Amen. (*Martyrdom of Polycarp* 14.1–3 [Kleist, p. 97])

But in any case, whether "prophetically" from the second century or actually—that is, etiologically—from a century later, Polycarp's prayer is consistent with what is found in other liturgical texts from the third century, such as, for example, the so-called Strasbourg Papyrus.[116]

Also significant is the way *The Martyrdom of Polycarp* fits in with a phenomenon that has been called, challengingly for those wedded to traditional historical assumptions, "the second church." As Ramsay MacMullen provocatively claims, archaeological evidence indicates that in the period from 200 CE to perhaps as late as 400 CE, it is likely that only a mere 5 percent of Christians regularly took part in the official worship of the Church. The other 95 percent? They participated in the highly popular cult of the martyrs that took place in cemeteries and tombs. In ceremonies apparently without the strict supervision of their bishops, who occasionally did complain about this,[117] Christians gathered to celebrate the memory of the heroic martyrs, to enter into union with them, and through them with Christ, and to receive from them the power, the strength, and the help they would need to live their lives both every day and in times of trial.[118] Robin Darling Young summarizes the significance of this:

> Of all early Christian practices, the veneration of the martyr-saints was the most popular and accessible. With a unanimity that eluded them in other matters of belief, Christians repeatedly gave three reasons for honouring these men and women as the most admirable and intensely exemplary of believers. First, the imitation of Christ enjoined on all believers appeared most visibly in their triumphant deaths. Second, in reward for their faithfulness, the martyrs now in heaven possessed special powers. And third, when Christians praised and supplicated them, the martyrs would return the favor of visible assistance. This complex rationale appears either

---

[116] See R. C. D. Jasper and G. J. Cuming, *Prayers of the Eucharist: Early and Reformed*, 3rd ed. (Collegeville, MN: Liturgical Press, 1987) 52–54.
[117] Cameron, *The Last Pagans of Rome* (see n. 3 in Foreword) *passim*, points out that much of this "complaining" was due to the frustrations of overly rigorous church authorities—not unlike the way some church figures in our own day complain about secularism and worldliness.
[118] MacMullen, *The Second Church* (see p. 9, n. 17 in Part 1).

implicitly or explicitly in numerous forms of literature attesting to early Christian martyrdom.[119]

In many ways, these Christians were doing, but precisely as Christians, the kinds of things that their non-Christian neighbors would be doing when they gathered to remember their dead and to share a common meal, the *refrigerium* (refreshment) which, in a Christian context, would come to include the Eucharist. Quite remarkably, therefore, *The Martyrdom of Polycarp*, our earliest clear evidence for the cult of the martyrs, is also witness, along with other documents of the same age, to the early Christian theology of sacrifice. And, in Polycarp's prayer it is also witness to an early form of what eventually became the classical eucharistic anaphora. Of further significance is that this document likely comes from the time of the Decian persecution, the time when the empire, qua empire and not just in local persecutions, was beginning to take seriously the presence and, as the empire perceived it, the threat of Christianity. It was actually, although not obvious at the time, an uneven battle, as became clear a century later when Christianity, although still a minority, had become not just a *religio licita* but one that enjoyed the favor and support of a series of Christian emperors. For the religio-psychological support that pious pagans in the general populace might get from offering sacrifice, or from feeling somehow included in the publicly offered sacrifices, the Christians at all levels—both their literate elite and their nonliterate masses—would get, and in a much more satisfying and powerful way, from participating in the cult of the martyrs.

But lest we assume there was no value in that from which the Christians were attempting to distance themselves, it is good to remind ourselves of the glowing terms in which Peter Brown could speak of "The Ancient Religion" that could still command the nostalgic loyalty of one so cultured as Symmachus (see 2.12., pp. 49–50) and the impressive antiquarian interest of one so learned as Macrobius (see 2.13., p. 51):

> The gods were not airy abstractions. They were beings, who hovered rank after rank above and around the human race. The lower orders of the gods shared the same physical space as human beings. They touched all aspects

---

[119] Robin Darling Young, "Martyrdom as Exaltation," in Denis R. Janz, ed., *A People's History of Christianity*, vol 2: *Late Ancient Christianity*, ed. Virginia Burrus (Minneapolis, MN: Fortress Press, 2005) 74–75, cited from Johnson, "Martyrs and the Mass" (see p. 11, n. 20) 4.

of the natural world and of human settlement. Not all gods were equal. Some gods were considerably higher and more distant from human beings than were others. The *religio* that these high gods received depended, to a large extent, on the self-image of their worshippers. Mystical philosophers yearned for the higher gods and, beyond them, for union with the One, the metaphysically necessary, intoxicating source of all being. Such high love for a distant god lifted the soul out of the body, in a manner which made all earthly cares fall silent. Philosophers yearned for union with the One High God.[120]

But ultimately, and in contrast, no pagan, at any level, could be much inspired by the idea of becoming one with or of imitating the pagan gods of mythic antiquity. Christian and other polemicists scored easy debate points on that score. But even when the never-very-numerous philosophers of the non-Christian literate elite developed "reasonable ideas of the divinity," and could talk approvingly about union with the divinity as the goal of theurgic sacrifice as we have seen in Iamblichus (see 2.10., pp. 39–46), the "debate" or, if you will, the discourse about sacrifice, was still uneven. For, as Robin Darling Young so eloquently explained, Christians of all classes, the non-elite masses as well as the relatively few literate elite, could agree on venerating the martyrs as models of how they, as Christians, were personally called to imitate Christ, on how the martyrs were possessors of and dispensers of special powers and favors, especially the power and courage to follow in a personal, bodily way, if called thereto, the example of Christ and the martyrs. The truly marvelous ways in which, for example, Iamblichus could talk about union with the gods/the divinity as the goal and purpose of theurgic sacrifice—let alone the relatively pale way in which Sallust later tried to pass on this teaching of Iamblichus—could not begin to approach the power of this specifically and uniquely Christian mode of sacrificial discourse.

t. The anaphoras of the fifth century

But let us now move from the age of the martyrs to the end of the fourth and beginning of the fifth century, and to the relatively mature and well-formed

---

[120] Brown, *The Rise of Western Christendom*, Tenth Anniversary Revised Edition (see p. 2, n. 3 in Part 1) 59.

Christian Eucharistic Prayers/anaphoras that began to appear at that time. Once again, the relative paucity of historical data on early Christian liturgical development does not allow us to trace this development on a year-to year or even decade-to-decade basis. For example, critical analysis of the data behind the brief remarks we made above in 3.3.*p.* (pp. 96–97) do not support traditional assumptions of a *linear* development. But there was development, and we can take the so-called anaphora of Chrysostom as a typical high point of it. Whether or not this anaphora was actually composed or used in its final form by the historical John of Antioch (Chrysostom) is not important here. For it has, in any case, been in use and associated with his name from the beginning of the fifth century. Whereas the early predecessors to this anaphora had, as we saw in the prayer of Polycarp, a relatively simple tripartite structure of (1) anamnesis/praise and thanksgiving, (2) epiclesis/supplication, and (3) final doxology, this structure is now considerably expanded. For even as early as this early-fifth-century Chrysostom anaphora we find all but one of the ten elements that, in five groups (**A–E**), give the basic structure that, with variations, is recognizably followed by most of the developed Eucharistic Prayers from that day to our own: **A** 1, Introductory Dialogue; **A** 2, Preface; **A** 3, Sanctus; **B** 4, Post-Sanctus; **B** 5, Preliminary Epiclesis; **C** 6, Narrative of Institution; **D** 7, Anamnesis; **D** 8, Epiclesis; **D** 9, Diptychs/Intercessions; **E** 10, Doxology.[121]

Upon examination, we find that all of the newer elements that are added to the earlier tripartite structure, with one striking exception, turn out to be different aspects of either anamnetic (praise/thanksgiving) or epicletic (supplication/petition) praying. The one striking exception is **C 6**, the Narrative of the Institution of the Eucharist. Within the Eucharistic Prayer, Jesus' eucharistic words, usually in the form of a selective conflation of Mk 14:22–25, Mt. 26:26–29, Lk. 22:17–23, and Paul (1 Cor. 1:23–25) are an "embolism," that is, an insertion into an already existing prayer structure. That they are an embolism is verified by the fact that they are inserted inconsistently into different Eucharistic Prayers, sometimes into the anamnetic part, sometimes into the epicletic part, and sometimes in or as the transition between the

---

[121] See W. Jardine Grisbrooke, "Anaphora," in *The New Dictionary of Liturgy and Worship*, ed. John G. Davies (London: SCM/Philadelphia, PA: Westminster, 1986) 13–21.

two parts. As biblical scholars have pointed out from their study of the early instances of such embolisms in the Hebrew Scriptures, the context of, and thus the reason for, the insertion of an embolism into a given prayer is critical for determining the meaning and function of that prayer in that particular context. Hence, for us, the question that jumps out at us is: Why, as far as we know, do none of the Eucharistic Prayers that have come to us from before the fourth century include the Narrative of Institution? And why do practically all the Eucharistic Prayers that have taken shape since the Council of Nicea in 325 have this embolism, this insertion into the Eucharistic Prayer of the explicit narrative of Jesus actually instituting the Eucharist?

One helpful answer, following the reasoning suggested by Maxwell Johnson (see p. 11, n. 20), is congenially revelatory. The context: *First*, the well-established Christian custom of thinking of and referring to the Eucharist as sacrificial—whether referring just to the prayer of the Eucharist or also to its ritual celebration—goes back to the early years. *Second*, the Christian custom of thinking of martyrdom as the ultimate participation in the sacrifice of Christ goes back at least to Ignatius of Antioch. As witnessed by *The Martyrdom of Polycarp*, the other acts of the martyrs, and the massive basilicas that the Constantinian and post-Constantinian emperors constructed over numerous cemetery sites to support the cult of the martyrs, this understanding of martyrdom had become both widespread and popular. But *third*, from the time of Constantine's supremacy, martyrdom and anti-Christian persecution had fairly well ceased to be part of the lived experience of Christians in the Roman Empire. It seems to be no coincidence that it was in this context, when the personal threat of, and challenge of, and thus opportunity for martyrdom was no longer part of everyday Christian existence, that the instituting eucharistic words of Jesus, along with their—by then—massive martyrological-sacrificial connotations, became an integral part of the then developing classical Eucharistic Prayers of the Great Church. In the time of the martyrs, the martyrological-sacrificial context and meaning of eucharistic praying was self-evident and needed no explicit mention. After that time, the power of Christian sacrificial rhetoric, no longer fueled by the actual threat or realistic possibility of martyrdom, could then still be kept alive by the specific highlighting and massive ritual emphasis now placed on Jesus' Words of Institution. We do not assume that this was the only dynamic at play in this development, or that it was due to any conscious, explicit, or widespread plan, but it does seem to offer one reasonable and in many ways quite satisfying explanation for what was actually taking place in the mid-to-late-fourth Christian century.

After the fourth century, the popularity of the cult of the martyrs faded, and most of the great basilicas built to support it also gradually disappeared, many of them becoming convenient quarries for other buildings. But the theology of martyrdom and its supporting sacrificial rhetoric became increasingly appropriated by Christians in a somewhat unifying way at all levels, both among the illiterate masses and among the literate elite. Pagan sacrifice was no longer supported and was, increasingly, even forbidden by the state. At the end of the fourth century, Symmachus and most of his pagan contemporaries of the senatorial class may well have been interested in continuing the public sacrifices as integral to their concept of the welfare of the state. But with no way in practice or in theory to unify their cause in the face of the increasing dominance of Christianity, and with the emperors—apart from Julian the Apostate (361–363)—aggressively favoring the Christian cause, pagan sacrifice, at least as a widely practiced public cult, increasingly faded into nonexistence.

Excursus 3: A trinitarian view of sacrifice

Early on,[122] we asserted that much recent historical-liturgical scholarship has been finding that the idea of sacrifice that was being projected back into antiquity by traditional history-of-religions research—the supposedly Christian idea of sacrifice that necessarily involves the destruction of a victim—is itself a misunderstanding of authentic Christian sacrifice. This raises two significant questions: *First*, and obviously, if that common viewpoint is indeed a misunderstanding, what is it that we are claiming to be authentic Christian sacrifice? The answer to this is important since it names the conscious bias with which I, although also committed to work within the bounds of historical-critical scholarship, have approached the writing of this book. *Then, second*, in order to justify this excursus, we need to answer the second question: Is what we claim to be the authentic Christian idea of sacrifice actually present in Antiquity?

---

[122] See Part 1.1. and especially Daly, *Sacrifice Unveiled* (p. viii, n. 1).

(1) In answer to the first question, authentic Christian sacrifice is a profoundly trinitarian event or reality that can be theologically described (as we have already indicated above in our preliminary note [pp. 53–58]) as follows:

> First of all, Christian sacrifice is not some object that we manipulate, nor is it something that we do or give up. It is first and foremost, a mutually self-giving event that takes place between persons. It is, in fact, the most profoundly personal and interpersonal event that we can conceive or imagine. It begins, in a kind of first "moment," not with us but with the self-offering of God the Father in the self-gift-sending of the Son. It continues, in a second "moment," in the self-offering "response" of the Son, in his humanity and in the power of the Holy Spirit, to the Father and for us. And it continues further in a third "moment"—and only then does it begin to become Christian sacrifice—when we, in and by means of human actions that are empowered by the same Spirit that was in Jesus, begin to enter into that perfect, en-Spirited, mutually self-giving, mutually self-communicating personal inter-relationship that is the life of the Blessed Trinity.[123]

(2) In answer to the second question, whether this explicitly trinitarian idea of sacrifice was actually present in antiquity, the answer is a nuanced yes. It was there at least virtually and implicitly. For there is little in this theological description of Christian sacrifice that was not already taught, in one way or another, by the Fathers of the Church, and affirmed by the ecumenical councils of the fourth and fifth centuries, and de facto lived by countless devout Christians since then. For our purposes, the clearest evidence for this is in the official eucharistic praying of the Church, that eucharistic praying of Christians, at least when led by one of their literate elite, when it was prayed—especially when combating Arianism—*to* the Father and *to* the Son and *to* the Holy spirit, or, in the form that eventually became more common, *to* the Father, *through* the Son, and *in* the Holy Spirit. The great Eucharistic Prayers/anaphoras of Basil, Chrysostom, and others of this period—early fifth century—illustrate this trinitarian mode of praying. A few pages ago (3.3.t., pp. 107–10) we outlined the structure of this prayer and highlighted the martyrological-sacrificial

---

[123] *Sacrifice Unveiled* (see p. viii, n. 1) 5. The scare quotes around the words "moment" and "response" are to alert/remind us that, strictly, there are no "moments"—no before or after—in the eternal life of the Trinity, nor is there any of the negative otherness or any of the opposition that can be suggested by the "response" of Jesus.

significance of Jesus' Eucharistic Words of Institution that were being inserted into all the Eucharistic Prayers taking shape from the fourth century on.

It is a prayer that, although proclaimed only by the presiding bishop or priest, is actually a prayer of the whole Christian assembly. For it is never to be prayed by the presider as a mere personal prayer or just in his own name, but always in the first person plural, representing the whole assembly, and indeed the whole Church, and usually beginning and ending in an emphatically trinitarian way. In the opening Preface of the Chrysostom anaphora we hear: "It is fitting and right to hymn you . . . you and your only-begotten Son and your Holy Spirit. . . . For all these things we give thanks to you and to your only-begotten Son and to your Holy Spirit." Then, in the opening words of the anaphora itself, we read/hear: "Holy are you and all-holy, and your only-begotten Son, and your Holy Spirit."[124] This leads to the first of two major high points, the embolism (insertion) of Jesus' Eucharistic Words of Institution with their massive martyrological-sacrificial connotations, which in turn leads in transition to the second high point, the epicletic section of the anaphora that entreats the Father to send the Spirit to transform the assembly into the ecclesial body of Christ and its gifts into the sacramental body and blood of Christ shed/sacrificed for the life of the world. In the closely related anaphora of Basil we hear the presider, still addressing the Father, pray:

> We pray and beseech you, O holy of holies, in the good pleasure of your bounty, that your Holy Spirit may come upon us and upon these gifts set forth, and bless them and sanctify and make this bread the precious body of our Lord and Savior Jesus Christ. Amen. And this cup the precious blood of our Lord and God and Savior Jesus Christ, which is shed for the life of the world. . . . Unite with one another all of us who partake of the one bread and the cup in fellowship with the one Holy Spirit.[125]

Then, after praying in some detail to the Father, understood through the Son and in the Holy Spirit, for the various needs of the Church and world, the prayer concludes:

---

[124] Jasper and Cuming, *Prayers of the Eucharist* (see p. 105, n. 116) 132.
[125] Ibid., 119–20.

And grant us with one mouth and one heart to glorify and hymn your all-honorable and magnificent name, the Father, the Son, and the Holy Spirit. Amen.[126]

After quoting our description of authentic Christian sacrifice as a trinitarian event, we then went on to claim that this specifically and profoundly trinitarian idea of sacrifice was actually, though perhaps only virtually and implicitly, present in Christian antiquity. To that quote in its original context we had in fact added the comment:

> In a nutshell, this is the whole story. Anything less than this, and especially anything other than this, is simply not *Christian* sacrifice. . . . It might be something that Christians do, or it might be something that some Christians think is sacrifice, but if it is not trinitarian in this sense, it is not *Christian* sacrifice.[127]

We can sum up the place in this book of this excursus and what it claims in the following five points. (1) We have seen how the earliest Christians saw sacrifice in spiritualized or metaphorical terms. They also, increasingly, spoke and wrote about the Eucharist as sacrificial, but it was not so much the ritual being performed but rather the prayer of the Eucharist that they saw as sacrificial. (2) We have also seen how the insertion of the Eucharistic Words of Institution into all the Eucharistic Prayers that were taking shape from about the middle of the fourth century, how this insertion massively emphasized the sacrificial nature of this prayer. (3) The effect on the participants was, ultimately, trinitarian divinization/theosis, for that is what is happening when one—see above, the third "moment" of our description of Christian sacrifice—"begin[s] to enter into that perfect, en-Spirited, mutually self-giving, mutually self-communicating inter-personal relationship that is the life of the Blessed Trinity."[128] It is noteworthy that should one—by way of thought experiment—prescind from the specifically Christological and trinitarian aspects of this Christian "mystery," what one has is not wholly unlike the communion with the Divinity that the Neoplatonist Iamblichus saw as the goal of sacrifice or

---

[126] Ibid., 134.
[127] Daly, *Sacrifice Unveiled* (see p. viii, n. 1) 5.
[128] For general background, see the recent work on deification by Norman Russell, Stephen Finlan, and Vladimir Kharlamov (p. 85, n. 66).

theurgic activity (see 2.10., pp. 39–46). (4) One must stress that while all the aspects of what we described at the beginning of this excursus may have actually been present in Christian antiquity, especially in that brilliant trajectory from Origen, through Athanasius and the Cappadocians and up to Cyril of Alexandria, no one in antiquity has been recorded as dotting the "i"s and crossing the "t"s to the extent that has now become possible to contemporary scholars.[129] (5) Finally, considering that so few Christians were regularly participating in the official worship of the Church, and that, as nearly as can be determined, so few would have been in a position to physically hear, let alone understand, the implications of the majestic anaphoras being prayed by at least some bishops at that time, we can only conjecture what most Christians explicitly thought about what they were doing—as opposed to what, at a pre-discursive level they "felt" or "knew" was taking place—when they convened in cemeteries and the basilicas built over them to venerate and become one with their Christ and with the Christian heroes that had gone before them and, in that context, to celebrate what their elite were calling "the sacrifice of the Church."

Excursus 4: The Eucharist as sacrifice

Among the earliest followers of Jesus, few, if any, would have, or, strictly speaking, even could have, thought of the Eucharist as sacrificial, let alone as "a sacrifice." That is not only because at that early time they had barely even begun to think of themselves as "Christian," a group separate from Judaism, but also because the terms "Eucharist" and "sacrifice" likewise did not yet exist as distinctive Christian realities. In addition, even when they had begun to be aware of themselves as Christian, their general, and, at times, because of persecution, quite painful awareness of their situation, was that sacrificing was

---

[129] I am referring specifically to the work of Kilmartin, *The Eucharist in the West* (see p. 3, n. 4) 381–83. See also my remarks on p. 7, n. 12 of *Sacrifice Unveiled* (see p. viii, n. 1): "In our opinion no book of similar scope has yet appeared that on the basis of the theological tradition of East and West offers such a systematic, consistently structured Trinitarian theology of Christian worship and sacrament"—Hans Bernhard Meyer, S.J., "Eine trinitarische Theologie der Liturgie und der Sakramente," *Zeitschrift für katholische Theologie* 113 (1991) 24–38, at 37, as quoted and translated by Michael A. Fahey, S.J., "In Memoriam: Edward J. Kilmartin, S.J., (1923-1994)," *Orientalia Christiana Periodica* 61 (1995) 5-35, at 17-18. Meyer is referring to Edward J. Kilmartin, S.J., *Christian Theology: Theology and Practice*. Part 1 *Systematic Theology of Liturgy* (Kansas City: Sheed & Ward, 1988).

what pagans did, or what Jews used to do in their now destroyed temple, but definitely not something that they themselves did. Nevertheless, by the time we come to the fifth century and to the end of the time period that frames this study, Christians, as we have seen, were not only routinely using sacrificial language and imagery in a metaphorical or spiritualized sense to describe their own Christian lives, they had also become comfortable with using the term "sacrifice" to describe the Eucharist, their central ritual prayer/action. Summarizing in a focused and much more nuanced way than did my earlier accounts of how this remarkable development came about is the purpose of this excursus.[130]

Our obvious starting point is the four New Testament accounts of Jesus instituting the Eucharist. In their probable chronological order of composition, they are: Paul's First Letter to the Cor. 11:23–26 (ca. 54 CE); Mk 14:22–25 (probably late 60s CE); Lk. 22:14–20 (probably mid-80s CE); Mt. 26:26–29 (probably late 80s CE). While none of these texts state that the Eucharist is a sacrifice, it seems clear that they all come from communities that were experiencing what we now call their Eucharists as celebrations laden with sacrificial meaning. For example, 1 Corinthians 10, the chapter just before the one in which Paul quotes the Institution Narrative, presupposes that Paul and his readers saw their Eucharistic celebration as a sacrifice of the communion type. A few decades later, the care taken by the writers of the synoptic gospels, Mark, Luke, and Matthew, to situate Jesus' Last Supper in the framework of the Passover celebration heightens the sacrificial connotations of that meal. For, the taken-for-granted way in which Paul had proclaimed in 1 Cor. 5:7 that "Christ our Passover Lamb has been sacrificed" suggests that, in the Pauline Communities, by the time we come to the mid-fifties of the first Christian century, the connection between Christ, Passover, and sacrifice had already become an established part of the tradition.

In addition, the instituting words themselves, that by the same mid-fifties were already taking the shape in which they have actually come down to us, contain several obvious sacrificial allusions: (a) the "blood of the (new) covenant" evokes the unique Exod. 24:3–8 covenant sacrifice; (b) "shed for

---

[130] My first treatments of this subject were in an appendix and in the final section of my first two books: pp. 498–508 of *Christian Sacrifice* and pp. 127–34 of *The Origins of the Christian Doctrine of Sacrifice* (see p. viii, n. 1).

you/for many" would remind the early Jewish Christians of the all-important blood rites of the Jewish animal sacrifices;[131] (c) the various "for you" and "for many" phrases implicitly evoke the sacrificial connotations of Christic Servant Christology; (d) the commemorative eucharistic command "Do this in memory of me" evokes the anamnetic motif of the Jewish Passover celebration that used to begin with the sacrificing of the lambs in the temple. While no single one of these would suffice to ground a solid claim that the first-century followers of Jesus saw their eucharistic celebrations as sacrificial, their cumulative effect makes that conclusion fairly obvious.

Supporting this conclusion is the *Didache*, a remarkable Christian church-order document that, at some time in the late first or early second century, had apparently been assembled from a variety of sources, both oral and written. Toward the end of that document we read that, in preparation for the weekly Lord's Day gathering for the breaking of the bread and offering of thanks, the faithful are exhorted to confess their sins "so that your sacrifice may be pure" (*Did* 14.1) and "lest your sacrifice be defiled" (*Did* 14.2), "your sacrifice" apparently referring to the whole ceremony. The next verse goes on to quote what subsequently becomes a favorite Early Christian quotation from the Old Testament. But that which, in its original form in Mal. 1:11 had been a *prophecy* is, here in *Didache* 14.3, rephrased into a *command* to offer pure sacrifice to the name of the Lord. However, while the existence of the idea of the Eucharist as sacrifice is thus confirmed, and even taken for granted, there is no indication of precisely what, near the end of the first Christian century, this actually meant. Whereas, earlier in *Didache* 9 and 10, we find two beautiful Eucharistic Prayers, neither of them contains a hint of anything sacrificial. And in any case they come from a much more primitive, even pre-gospel and pre-Christological stratum of sources, and thus cannot be used to flesh out the meaning of "your sacrifice" in *Didache* 14.1 and 2.[132]

Clement of Rome (fl. ca. 96 CE) uses sacrificial language to describe both the public life of the Church and its liturgy. His *First Epistle* (*1 Clement* 44.3–4)

---

[131] Recall how the Epistle to the Hebrews repeats the rabbinic dictum: "Without the shedding of blood there is no forgiveness of sins" (Heb. 9:22).

[132] For a full treatment of the *Didache*, see Milavec, *The Didache* (see p. 80, n. 53); idem, *The Didache: Text, Translation, Analysis, and Commentary* (Collegeville, MN: Liturgical Press, 2003). For a quick review of various scholarly views on the *Didache*, see van de Sandt, ed., *Matthew and the Didache* (see p. 81, n. 53).

sees the bishop as having a sacrificial function in the Church's worship. But even when Clement speaks of this function as "offering the sacrifices" (44.4), he seems to be using sacrifice mostly in the spiritualized sense of the *prayer* of praise and thanksgiving. The context, at that very early date, does not suggest that we interpret these sacrifices/gifts as referring primarily to the eucharistic elements of bread and wine.

The letters that Ignatius of Antioch (ca. 35–ca. 107 CE) wrote on his way to martyrdom in Rome do not, strictly speaking, write of the Eucharist as sacrifice. That idea, however, is at least implicitly and indeed powerfully in the background, especially in his *Epistle to the Romans* when he looks ahead to his martyr's death in terms both liturgical and sacrificial: "That I be sacrificed to God while the altar is still prepared" (*Ign. Rom.* 2.2). Then, later in that Epistle, the sacrifice-Eucharist connection is more than just alluded to when Ignatius speaks of being "the wheat of God" and of becoming "the pure bread of Christ" so that "by these things I may be found a sacrifice" (*Ign. Rom.* 4.1–2).

Several decades later, with the apologist, *Justin Martyr* (ca. 100–ca. 165), what had hitherto been only implicit was becoming more explicit: *Christian sacrifice is the Eucharist*. As for what Justin understands by that, the key passage—also consistent with everything else he says about sacrifice and Eucharist—is from his (ca. 156 CE) *Dialogue with Trypho*:

> Now, that prayers and giving thanks, when offered by worthy men, are the only perfect and pleasing sacrifices to God, I also admit. For such sacrifices are what Christians alone have undertaken to offer, and they do this in the remembrance effected by their solid and liquid food whereby the suffering endured by the Son of God is brought to mind. (*Trypho* 117.3)

Thus, as with earlier Christian witnesses, Justin's idea of Christian sacrificial activity remains primarily the spiritualized sacrifice of prayerful praise and thanksgiving. But in addition, it is now especially associated with the eucharistic celebration. In sum, we can say that Christian sacrifice, even at this early date, was already in the process of becoming the prayer of praise and thanksgiving pronounced over, or before, or on the occasion of the offering of the eucharistic bread and cup. Nevertheless, it needs to be emphasized that, apart from what Christians of a later age could and did confidently read into Justin's words,[133] there is insufficient evidence to conclude unambiguously that, then in the mid-second century, his idea of Christian sacrificial activity *specifically* did include—as it obviously could for Christian readers of later centuries—consecratory action over the gifts of bread and wine.

Irenaeus of Lyons (ca. 130–ca. 200 CE) intensifies the "development"[134] we saw taking place in Justin. He speaks of the eucharistic bread and cup as "the new oblation of the new covenant."[135] In calling this Eucharist the "offering of the church" (*Adv. Haer.* 4.31.1–3) he goes into greater detail and says much more than did Justin, especially in emphasizing the words of Christ spoken over the bread and the cup. But now, Eucharist means not only prayers; it also emphatically includes the good dispositions, works, and lives of the Christian faithful. Thus, as it had been with Justin, it was still not so much in its cultic action—although that was indeed more emphasized in Irenaeus than in Justin—but more precisely in its prayers and thanksgivings that the Eucharist was a sacrifice.

In Hippolytus of Rome (ca. 170–236 CE) we find a concept of sacrifice that, negatively speaking, is relatively free of the polemical concerns that preoccupied Justin (against the Jews) and Irenaeus (against the heretics/gnostics) and that, positively speaking, is characterized by an intensely realistic, physical conception of the self-offering of the Word Incarnate. The connection between incarnation and sacrifice becomes the leitmotif of his theology of sacrifice. We find perhaps the strongest expression of this in Hippolytus's homily against the Patripassian heresy of Noetus (ca. 200):

> Will he say that flesh was not in heaven? Yet there is the flesh which was presented by the Word of the Father as an offering, the flesh that came forth

---

[133] Chapter 67 of Justin's *First Apology* is often appealed to as an early witness for the later doctrine of metabolic real presence: "Not as common bread and common drink do we receive these ... the food which is blessed by the prayer of his [Jesus Christ] word ... is the flesh and blood of that Jesus who was made flesh." But a careful reading of Justin's Greek reveals that the transformation/consecratory action spoken of here is not so much what takes place in/to the bread and wine but what takes place in the Christians receiving this Eucharist.

[134] The scare quotes around "development" are to remind us that, although we take care to place these Early Christian sources in their approximate chronological order, that does not imply that the later authors were always actually aware of and consciously building on everything their Christian predecessors thought and wrote. See, for example, Daly, "Eucharistic Origins" (p. 72, n. 36).

[135] Irenaeus, *Adversus Haereses* 4.29.5.

from the Spirit and the Virgin and was shown to be the perfect Son of God. It is evident, therefore, that he offered himself to the Father. Before this there was no flesh in heaven.[136]

By this point, "Eucharist as sacrifice" is beginning to take on a level of complexity that tends to delegitimize brief, broad-brushed treatments of it such as we attempt here. In my attempt to say something helpful, I will rely on some of the summarizing statements in David N. Power's magisterial *The Eucharistic Mystery*.[137] First, Power notes that even this early, still in the pre-Nicene period, there was already some "sacerdotalization of ministry" and the beginning of "a more cultic view of the Eucharist."[138] This "cultic turn" (Power 118) was the beginning of something that eventually, especially in the infelicitous quarrels of the Reformation and Counter-Reformation, developed into serious problems. But here, as we enter into what has been referred to as the golden age of patristic theology, things were still in some kind of balance. For example, in the West Syrian Eucharistic Prayers of Basil and Chrysostom, the eucharistic offerings/eucharistic gifts seem to include both the bread and wine *and* the prayer of the Church over them. And at the same time, in the East Syrian tradition, the ceremony of Eucharistic sacrifice was adding a "new stress on the propitiatory character of Christ's death and . . . its eucharistic commemoration" (Power 140–41). By this time (early fifth century) the term "sacrifice" was "apparently used to refer to the Eucharistic action as a whole, including the commemoration prayers of thanksgiving and intercession, the devotion of the people, *and* [my emphasis] the bread and wine that are proffered for blessing" (Power 142).

Power brilliantly summarizes the complexity of the post-Nicene understanding of Christian worship:

> It draws together (1) the commemoration of Christ's passion, death, and resurrection, (2) Christian ethical action, (3) the prayerful blessing of earth's gifts, and (4) prayers of praise, thanksgiving, and intercession, all of this

---

[136] Hippolytus, *Against Noetus* 4. Translated from E. Schwartz, *Zwei Predigten Hippolyts* (Sitzungsberichte der Bayerischen Akademie der Wissenschaften 3; 1936) 89. For a full English translation, see *Ante-Nicene Fathers* 5.223–31.

[137] David N. Power, *The Eucharistic Mystery: Revitalizing the Tradition* (New York: Crossroad, 1997) see especially 114–18; 140–43; 153–55. For more extensive background and treatment, see Daniel J. Sheerin, *The Eucharist; Message of the Fathers of the Church* 7 (Wilmington, DE: Michael Glazier, 1986), and Kenneth W. Stevenson, *Eucharist and Offering* (New York: Pueblo Publishing Company, 1986).

[138] See especially Cyprian's *Letter* 63 on the aquarian controversy, as well as several passages in the *Apostolic Tradition* (now generally seen as coming to us via the hand of a later, post-Nicene Arian redactor).

reaching a climax at the communion table of Christ's body and blood. To predicate offering or sacrifice of this complex reality is to interpret it by use of an image taken from a different kind of context [i.e., pagan animal sacrifice], one however that has already picked up considerable resonance in biblical stories and prophecies. . . . to be emphasized, however, is that [in contrast somewhat to what seemed be developing in the Roman and East Syrian traditions] the soteriology of Eucharistic prayers, whether before or after Nicea, is not dominantly that of propitiatory sacrifice. (as adapted from Power 143)

Much of this is impressively summed up in Augustine's "more sophisticated teaching in the *City of God*" where in 10.6 "Augustine defines sacrifice as works of mercy done towards self or neighbor through which access is had to God in holy communion (*sancta societas*)."[139] In the rest of Book 10 of the *City of God* Augustine expands the pithiness of this "definition," not eliminating the cultic but moving far beyond the merely cultic in order to stress the Christological, ecclesiological, and eschatological reality of Christian sacrifice. In Augustine's understanding it is the union of all Christians in Christ the head, incorporating into his eucharistic offering their daily spiritual sacrifices and works of mercy, and all of this—continuing in the West what Chrysostom and Theodore of Mopsuestia had been teaching in the East—being made perfect with Christ's ascension to God's right hand where he continues his priestly sacrificial mediation. Thus, as Power puts it, actually summing up most of the development of the tradition as a whole (except for the relative neglect in the West of the role of the Holy Spirit): "On both sacramental reality and sacrificial reality there is no way of separating Augustine's discourse on Christ from his discourse on the church" (Power 155).

---

[139] Power, *The Eucharistic Mystery* (see p. 119, n. 137) 154; see 3.3.*q*., p. 100.

Part Four

Select Points of Comparison and Contrast

After the Introduction, the two main parts of this book, Parts Two and Three, have had a predominantly historical or diachronic structure. Now, in Part Four, with that background in mind, we switch back to a predominantly systematic or synchronic structure in order, with an even broader brush, to offer some contemporary reflection on "Sacrifice in Pagan and Christian Antiquity" by way of seven select points of comparison and contrast: (1) prayer and sacrifice; (2) divination and sacrifice; (3) ethics, morality, and sacrifice; (4) the purpose of sacrifice; (5) the rhetoric of sacrifice; (6) the "economics" of sacrifice; (7) heroes and saints. Each of these points is as "actual" today as they were in Antiquity.

1 Prayer and sacrifice

Like the word "sacrifice," the modern word "prayer" has no precise correspondence in the ancient languages of the Mediterranean and Middle Eastern world. But, needing to begin somewhere, we can use the following descriptive definition of prayer in Antiquity:

> Every form of [spoken-aloud] speech . . . , with which the human being seeks to gain the help or support of a higher power, and which is normally accompanied by certain gestures, behaviors, and cultic actions.[1]

In the ancient world there seems to have been no unified ritually determined basic form of prayer and, in contrast to what was beginning to take shape in the monotheistic religions, no unified formulations of religious faith, although

---

[1] Daniel Jakov and Emmanuel Voutiras et al., "Gebet, Gebärden und Handlungen des Gebets," in *ThesCRA* 6.b (see p. 1, n. 2) vol. 3, pp. 107–79, at 107.

the Romans, unlike the Greeks, did favor set formulations in their praying. Spontaneous or free-standing prayer was not unknown and, among the popular masses, may not have been totally different from spontaneous praying among the Christian non-elite masses. But in the public sphere, prayer and sacrifice were so interconnected that there was no sacrifice without prayer and, for the most part, or at least very often, prayer would be accompanied by sacrifice or some other ritual action. In other words, prayer in Antiquity tended to be what we would call ritual speech. It not only expressed in words the action that was being performed; it was also, itself, performative. In Roman religion, for example, prayer could even be seen as more important than action. For the action, if necessary, could be repeated, while the words could not. Thus great precision was needed regarding the names of the deities being invoked, the beneficiaries of the ritual, and the exact formulations of precisely what the beneficiaries wanted. In other words, the prayer that accompanied sacrifice, and that indeed accompanied every significant human action involving a ritual, had to be an oral and detailed description of the concrete act.

In contrast to the Christian cult where prayer played an important role as a means of approach to a God who, like a merciful father, cares for his people,[2] the pagan world, at least the elite of the pagan world, generally understood the divine and human spheres to be quite separate realms. See above, pp. 106–7, Peter Brown's sympathetic description of the *religio* of the pagan world. There, the experience of prayer was an appeal to gods who generally came across to their devotees as, yes, powerful persons, but also as distant, and not necessarily interested persons. The main purpose of prayer, especially in the Roman religion of the imperial period, was to maintain the undisturbed coexistence of two separate worlds, the human and the divine, the so-called *pax deorum* that was so important to someone like Symmachus (see pp. 49–50) because that alone could assure the well-being of the Roman state.

Christian prayer, especially as related to sacrifice, was totally different. From the outset, and especially after the time of Christianity's definitive break with Judaism around the time of the ca. 70 CE destruction of the Jerusalem Temple,

---

[2] Recall the words of Jesus: "Is there any one among you who, if your child asks for bread, will give a stone? Or if the child asks for a fish, will give a snake? If you, then, who are evil, know how to give good gifts to your children, how much more will your Father in heaven give good things to those who ask him!" (Mt. 7: 9–11).

there was no Christian sacrificial action whatsoever, nothing that could in any fair assessment even be construed as a specifically Christian *ritual* sacrificial action. The communal prayer that the Christians came to call the Eucharist, was itself, and *precisely as prayer*, the sacrificial "action." Only gradually, in the course of the first few Christian centuries, did Christian eucharistic praying come to be seen as a ritual that, along with Christian lives of love and service could commonly be called sacrificial or even "a sacrifice."

2 Divination and sacrifice

In polytheistic antiquity, divination was the primary means by which human beings tried to fill their needs and desires for some understanding of what was happening in the present, and for some knowledge of, or at least for some assurance about, the future. Cicero's 44 BCE *De divinatione* distinguished between the *natural* divination that took place by way of privileged or direct communication with the gods, and the artificial divination that took place by way of the technical expertise of particularly skilled experts. *Artificial* divination, susceptible, as it often was, to political control or exploitation, came about largely as the side effect of a sacrificial offering such as examining the entrails of a sacrificial animal, which side effect was often the very purpose for which the sacrifice was offered in the first place. That close connection with bloody animal sacrifice was one of the obvious reasons why divination and its associated practices were rejected—and have stayed rejected until today— by Judaism, Christianity, and Islam. But divination, we must remember, was not just about the future. For our purposes it is helpful to use the wider understanding of divination and its purposes suggested by Waldner: "Its concern was to come to know and interpret the working of the gods in the world. It thus brought about communication not only *about*, but also *with* the world of the invisible."[3]

In other words, because of its identification with sacrifice, divination also involved communion with the gods or, as Paul put it in 1 Cor. 10:14–21, "with demons." It is no surprise then that divination, along with incense

---

[3] Katharina Waldner, "Märtyrer als Propheten: Divination und Martyrium im christlichen Diskurs des ersten und zweiten Jahrhunderts," in Hubert Cancik and Jörg Rüpke, *Die Religion des Imperium Romanum: Koine und Konfrontation* (Tübingen: Mohr Siebeck, 2009) 299–311, at 299.

offerings and animal sacrifice, was, at the insistence of the Christians, among the practices that the late-fourth-century Christian emperors most specifically tried to outlaw. For ultimately, it was not a battle over some distant or even imminent future, but *a battle over control in the here-and-now present*. The Christian bishops, for example, in true *vaticinium-ex-eventu*[4] style, liked to appeal to the Old Testament prophecies in order to "prove" why it was that the Christians were winning and the pagans were losing.

In terms of Antiquity-Christianity interaction, one of the more striking instances of divination was when, in 302 CE, according to Lactantius,[5] the emperor Diocletian who was the one actually arguing for milder means, and Galerius[6] who was arguing for extermination, sent a messenger to the oracle of Apollo at Didyma to resolve their differences about how to deal with "the Christian problem." When the messenger reported back that "the just on earth" were hindering Apollo's ability to speak, and Diocletian's advisors persuaded him that these "just on earth"—or "profane," as another text has it[7]—referred to the Christians, he was moved to unleash the final great persecution. It ended, ironically, a few years later with the legalization of Christianity and, a few decades after that with the first of, eventually, many proscriptions of animal sacrifice and divination. For serious-minded religious pagans it was also painfully ironic that, by this time, the oracular sanctuaries, because of an evolution taking place within pagan thinking and attitudes,[8] already seemed to be in decline. However, the repetition, over several centuries, of laws and decrees prohibiting animal sacrifice suggests that it had continued to be practiced, at least by some.

To sum up, divination, in the strict sense, seemed to have no place in official Christianity and in the writing and thinking of its literate elite. But that does not mean that Christians had no horse in this race. For Christians were very much involved in the same struggle in which the pagans found divination helpful, that is, in the struggle to understand and control the present and

---

[4] *Vaticinium-ex-eventu* is a common Latin phrase used to describe the rhetorical device of presenting as prophecy what one knows to have already taken place.
[5] *De mortibus persecutorum* 10.6–11.
[6] Galerius had been appointed coadjutor by Diocletian whom he succeeded in 305. His anti-Christian policies failed and he issued an edict of toleration shortly before his own death in 311.
[7] In Eusebius, *Vita Constantini* 2.50, it is "the profane on earth."
[8] See ThesCRA 6.a (see above, p. 1, n. 2) vol. 3, p. 94.

its implications for who will be in charge in the future. Waldner's relatively broad, present-oriented description of the purpose of divination that we just quoted enables us to see that that which the pagans were trying to achieve by divination, the Christians were trying to achieve in their own way, with, on the one hand, their bishops appealing *vaticinium-ex-eventu* style to Old Testament prophecy to support their apologetic claims, and with, on the other hand, the great popularity among the Christian populace, of an extensive and sometimes quite imaginative apocryphal and apocalyptic literature.

3 Ethics, morality, and sacrifice

Beginning with Hesiod's *Works and Days* (see 2.1., pp. 24–26) it was not unusual for those writing about sacrifice in the Graeco-Roman world to connect it to morality. But that relationship remained, at least in practice, undeveloped, vague, and imprecise. There was nothing, for example, that approached the Hebrew prophets' visceral rejection of all sacrifice that was not accompanied by the appropriate religious and moral dispositions of justice, mercy, and fraternal reconciliation. So fierce was this prophetic insistence that many readers and interpreters of the Bible have erroneously assumed that the Hebrew-prophetical critique of sacrifice was rejecting sacrifice itself. But then, as Judaism was approaching the Christian era, it was already going through a religious development that had begun to relativize the practice of ritual sacrifice. Subsequently, after the destruction of the temple in 70 CE, Judaism actually had to make do without sacrifice. Forced to make sense of a strong tradition that made both atonement and general well-being dependent on sacrifice, along with actual situations—exile, diaspora, and loss of the temple—the only place where legitimate sacrifice could be offered—that made sacrifice impossible, Judaism intensified its already ongoing spiritualization of sacrifice. What now, in Jewish thinking, made sacrifice effective was not the performance itself of the ceremony but the fact that it was performed in obedience to the will and law of God. This fulfilled in an unintendedly literal way the oft-repeated plea of Yahweh: "Obedience, not sacrifice." A variety of good works and holy actions like prayer, almsgiving, study of the Torah, fraternal correction and forgiveness, and so forth were substituted for sacrifice and seen as accepted by God as effectively sacrificial. This way of thinking was enthusiastically inherited/appropriated by the Christians and made the lynchpin of their own theology of sacrifice. For example, all five of the New Testament passages that directly mention Christian sacrificial activity are, taken in context, talking about ethical, not ritual, activity.[9] Thus, Christians did not just substitute for ritual sacrifice, they completely dispensed with the ritual altogether. There was nothing at all like this in the religious practices of the Greeks and Romans. Granted, some of the Stoics and Neoplatonists took moral positions that relativized sacrifice or, while dispensing with it in principle, left it in place and actually supported it as an external sign of their allegiance to the emperor. But none of them, and few if any of the other non-Christian critics of sacrifice made the move that the Jews made in so explicitly tying the effectiveness of sacrifice to morality, or that the Christians did in making the absolutizing and, in effect, politically subversive move of rejecting ritual sacrifice altogether. And none of them did anything like what the Christians did in appropriating the language and imagery of ritual animal sacrifice to express the central meaning of their lives.

It should be noted, however, that taking sacrifice as one's point of comparison is not a totally fair way to compare the morality and ethics of Antiquity and Christianity. For, as many have pointed out, there are numerous traces in antiquity of a widespread belief in the gods' concern with moral behavior. But it was the philosophers and not the religious authorities, and above all not those responsible for the sacrifices, who attempted to develop this idea. The normal assumption was that the favor of the gods was obtained simply by the proper performance of the proper rituals. Moral instruction was not the duty of priests or religious authorities. What connections were being made between morality and cult were being made by the philosophers, but with little apparent effect on popular thinking and practice.[10] Roman religion was "a religion with no moral code."[11] Or, expressed in strongly negative terms:

> Except for the emperor cult that, in its turn, was restricted to its function as loyalty religion and religious connection to the center of things, in the

---

[9] Rom. 12:1-2; Rom. 15:15-16; 1 Pet. 2:10; Heb. 10:19-25; Heb. 12:18-13:16. See above, pp. 78-79.
[10] See, for example, J. B. Rives, *Religion in the Roman Empire* (Malden, MA: Blackwell, 2007) 51-52.
[11] John Scheid, *An Introduction to Roman Religion* (Bloomington/Indianapolis, IN: Indiana University, 2003) 19 = ET (trans. Janet Lloyd) of *La Religion des Romans* (Paris, 1998).

Roman Empire the interest in religion was only in an empty power ritual devoid of ethics and personal engagement for the individual.[12]

Finally, it must be honestly admitted, and indeed emphasized, that this "story" is one that comes to us primarily through the apologetically colored lenses of the Christian literate elite. The Jews effectively passed on to Christians the teaching of their ideal of "obedience, not sacrifice." But did the Jews themselves, and as a whole, effectively live out that ideal in practice? And did the Christians themselves, and as a whole, effectively live it out in accordance with the elevated teaching of Jesus that their bishops were preaching? We can raise these questions, but, as Christians, conscious of ourselves being part of the "story" being told, we are not confident of being able to give "objectively" fair answers to them.[13]

4 The purpose of sacrifice

In the anthropomorphism common to the writings that have come to us from early antiquity, the purpose of sacrifice was usually to gain the favor of the gods who were thought somehow to have a need or desire for the sacrifices offered to them. The language of the biblical story of Noah's sacrifice after the flood in Gen. 8:20–21 suggests that similar ideas were also present at least in the early stages of Israelite biblical history. Later, by the time of late biblical Judaism and on the eve of the Christian era, the critical thinking at least of the literate elite, both Jewish and Graeco-Roman, had developed considerably. Under the influence of the Hebrew prophets on the one hand, and of the Greek philosophers on the other, the purpose of sacrifice was then thought to be of benefit more to human beings than to the gods or the Divinity. But there was also a significant difference. In the Judaism out of which Christianity grew, there had developed a very strong sense, actually a desperately strong sense, that the primary purpose of sacrifice was atonement: to ask God to restore (or strengthen) the divine-human relationship that had been disturbed by

---

[12] Christoph Auffarth, "Reichsreligion und Weltreligion," in Herbert Cancik et al., *Die Religion des Imperium Romanum* (see p. 123, n. 3) 37–54, at 37.

[13] See, for example, Ramsay MacMullen, *Christianity and Paganism in the Fourth to Eighth Centuries* (New Haven: Yale University, 1997); Harold A. Drake, "Intolerance, Religious Violence, and Political Legitimacy in Late Antiquity," *Journal of the American Academy of Religion* 79, no. 1 (2011) 193–235.

human sin. Except for the idea of the *pax deorum*, little or nothing of the kind can be found in the thinking or writing about sacrifice in the Graeco-Roman world. Thus when Theophrastus (ca. 300 BCE) listed three reasons for offering sacrifice: to give honor to the gods, to give them thanks, and to petition them for one's needs,[14] Jews (and later, Christians) mutatis mutandis, could have agreed with him, but only by also emphasizing that atonement was the overriding need for which they, in their sacrifices and prayers, needed to petition.

But structurally, Theophrastus's list comfortably fits into the fundamental bipartite structure—anamnetic/epicletic—of Jewish and Christian praying, and hence also of the basic structure underlying the Christian Eucharistic Prayer. Analogously, and once again mutatis mutandis, there is a remarkable similarity between the atonement purpose of sacrifice for Jews and Christians and, for the Graeco-Romans, the maintenance of the *pax deorum* that became so important to pagan thinking about sacrifice in the imperial period. But the "difference" in this particular analogy—and here it is a great difference—concerns ethics and morality. For Jews and Christians, ethical failings/sin is what makes atonement necessary, and sacrificing/praying with the proper ethical dispositions is what makes sacrificial atonement possible. For the pagans, ethics or morality was not totally unimportant but, as we have seen,[15] it did not have to be part of the sacrifices or of the religious rituals that were needed to maintain the *pax deorum*.

A further point about which there is striking convergence, at least among the literate elites as one approaches high and late antiquity, is the idea of communion with the Deity as a major—indeed *the* major purpose of sacrifice. Iamblichus, as we have seen (pp. 39–46), develops this at length in his specifically Neoplatonic way, and the Church Fathers do the same in their own Christianizingly Neoplatonic way as they speak, sometimes implicitly and sometimes explicitly, about the divinization/theosis that is the purpose and goal of Christian praying and Christian participation in the Eucharistic sacrifice.[16]

In other words, among the more gifted of the elite in pagan and Christian Antiquity, there was a remarkable convergence of understanding about the

---

[14] See pp. 29–32.
[15] See Part 2., pp. 21–51, *passim*, and Part 4.3., pp. 125–27, "Ethics, Morality, and Sacrifice."
[16] On divinization, see the works of Russell, Finlan, and Kharlamov listed on p. 85, n. 66.

purpose of sacrifice in particular and of religious ritual in general. The pagan elite, primarily by way of Neoplatonic philosophical reasoning, and the Christian elite, primarily by way of Judaeo-Christian revelation *and* theological reflection using a Neoplatonic philosophical toolbox, came, mutatis mutandis, to remarkably similar ideas about communion with God/the Divinity—see "theurgy" for Iamblichus, and "mystagogy" for the Christian Neoplatonists—as the final purpose of properly offered sacrifice.

5 The rhetoric of sacrifice

To be Roman or to be considered loyal to Rome did not necessarily involve any doctrine or religious belief. Instead of that it meant, as far as religion was concerned, simply to sacrifice or to allow oneself to be at least externally connected to sacrificing in a variety of specified and ritually controlled ways. The Christian refusal to go along with this was, to the mind of the Romans, puzzling, and to their political sense, perversely subversive. Thus the battleground between Christians and Romans, or, more precisely, when the relationships between them became a battleground,[17] tended to center on the practice of ritual sacrifice. Both had developed a discourse that ritualized their conflicting understandings of how the cosmos functioned: on one side the ritual sacrifices necessary for maintaining the empire-supporting *pax deorum*, and on the other side the spiritual sacrifices of Christians living and dying that signified for them the growing presence of the *pax Christi* and the kingdom of God. In other words, both sides "understood 'sacrifice' and ritualized it in various ways as expressions of power and identity."[18] But looked at in this way, that is, not just in its historical outcome but specifically in its inner rhetoric, the battle was uneven. As Heyman expressed it:

> In place of the social control ritually portrayed in imperial sacrifices uniting the center and periphery, Christianity ritualized Jesus' sacrificial death

---

[17] Most of the time, and in most places, the Christians seemed to coexist peacefully with their pagan neighbors. See, for example, the extensive work of Cameron, *The Last Pagans of Rome* (see p. ix, n. 3) *passim*.

[18] Heyman, *The Power of Sacrifice* (see p. 6, n. 12) 210. But note here Ullucci's massive critique of Heyman's position recorded above, p. 19.

through Eucharist and baptism in the life of each believer. Just as the emperor and the imperial family were exalted along the "sliding scale of divinity," so too the Christian martyr shared (as much as theologically possible) in the exalted status of the risen Jesus. Just as Rome portrayed power and imperial benefits through ritual sacrifice, the martyrs' second baptism of blood infused them with power to do battle with the forces of Satan. However, unlike the Roman model, where only the emperor was apotheosized after his death, *all* Christians, especially those called by God to martyrdom, were guaranteed the reward of heaven.[19]

It is interesting to speculate how different the outcomes might have been had the playing field been level, had not all the emperors since Constantine, save for Julian's two years, not been Christian, had the attempts of the philosophers to connect morality with ritual not been so ineffectual, or had the attempts of some of the mystery religions to bring personal conversion and engagement to the practice of religion enjoyed aggressive imperial support—except for Julian's brief reign in AD 361–63—the way Christianity did. How much of what seems to be the obvious superiority of the Christian rhetoric might be due to the fact that Christians have been almost the only ones who "survived" to tell this story?

6 The "economics" of sacrifice

Ritual sacrifice inevitably involves not just the question of what to sacrifice, to whom, and for what purpose, but also the question of how much to offer and ultimately, and in some ways most importantly: who gets what? It is far more complicated than the simplistic: "The larger the better." Right from the outset of the literary period, as we see in Hesiod's *Theogony*, we find concern about which gods get how much of what was offered; in other words, concern about the apportionment and consumption aspects of sacrifice, the pervasive issue of the division and distribution of power, benefits, blessings, and sacrificial shares both among the gods and their human beneficiaries.[20]

---

[19] Ibid., 235.
[20] See Part 2.1. "Homer and Hesiod," pp. 21–26.

Hesiod's exhortation in *Works and Days* to sacrifice "according to your means" is but an early part of a long line of teaching—Socrates, Anaximenes, Jesus, and various representatives of both the Christian and non-Christian literate elites—that the appropriateness of and the dispositions with which one offers counts as much if not more than the size or grandeur of the offering.

But how does the "economics" of sacrifice work when a whole group rejects ritual material sacrifice? Christians dealt with this in two ways. First, they had already learned from the Jews that almsgiving and charitable care for those in need are prominent among those activities that, in a spiritualizing way, take the place of material sacrifices, and actually provide all the salvific benefits that used to come from them. Second, prayer, and most especially the unique, and over the centuries increasingly ritualized, Eucharistic Prayer became the specific *sacrificium Christianorum*, as Augustine put it. As part of their eucharistic celebrations, most of the Christian churches developed the practice of the offertory procession, the bringing forward of gifts and "offerings" for the support of the needy.[21]

However, long preceding this Christian practice was the "euergetism" (literally, the benefactorial "good-workism") of broadly shared public feasting on the sacrificial meats. Along with what was usually the primary religious motivation, the desire to appear pious, the desire also to appear generous seems to have been a significant motivating factor in the minds of donors or patrons of the sacrifices, whether private or public. This "show" factor was so important that "the much-expected sacrifice (because of the feast which followed) could often be delayed in favour of the procession."[22] This is, of course, distinct from the apparent (and for some Christians problematic—see 1 Cor. 8–9) practice that meat for sale in the markets may have originated as part of a sacrifice. This, as well as the procession-sacrifice-banquet custom was obviously the cause of tension between pagans and Christians, but there is not much evidence to suggest that this, specifically, was a major cause of such tension.

---

[21] See Edward J. Kilmartin, S.J., "Offerings," in Everett Ferguson, ed. *Encyclopedia of Early Christianity*, 2nd ed. (New York/London: Garland Publishing, 1997) 2.827–28.

[22] See Petropoulou, *Animal Sacrifice* (see p. 6, n. 12) 85.

7 Heroes and saints

With regard to pagan and Christian ceremonies concerning the dead, the superficial and often overemphasized similarities are, upon closer examination, exceeded by more profound dissimilarities. For there were vastly different conceptions of the afterlife, of the relationship of life in this world to life (if at all) in the next, and vastly different senses or feelings of personal relationship between those—whether pagan heroes or Christian saints—who had gone before and those actually still living in this world.[23]

Both pagans and Christians honored with a cult those who had impressed humanity with acts of physical or moral heroism. In late pagan antiquity this was due not only to the reaction to the rising tide of the Christian cult of the martyrs, but also to internal developments, especially in the Greek cult of the sage and, in the postclassical era, in the cult of Plato celebrated in Rome as well as in Athens. It was, for example, through his exegesis of Plato that Plotinus was thought to have achieved sanctity. As for Apollonius (see above, pp. 33–34), "even those worshipping him had a share in his divinity."[24] Similar ideas were associated with the deification of the emperor Julian, who, in the minds of many non-Christians, was actually thought of more as a Neoplatonic saint or sage than as a deified Roman emperor.[25]

But in ancient Christianity, as also sensed by its non-Christian contemporaries—who looked with abhorrence at Christians gathering at tombs and cemeteries, and at their love of physical contact with the bodily remains of the martyrs—something radically different was taking place. "The imaginative boundaries . . . between heaven and earth, the divine and the human, the living and the dead, the town and its antithesis"[26] were being erased. In countless obviously visible places all over the empire, all over the Mediterranean world, where tomb and altar were being joined, Christian cultic places were becoming places where heaven and earth met. And "in a relic, the chilling anonymity of human remains could be thought to be still

---

[23] For the pagans, see *ThesCRA* II, 3.d (see p. 1, n. 2) "Heroisierung und Apotheose," pp. 125–214. For an overview of the Christian scene, see Peter Brown, *The Cult of the Saints* (London: SCM/Chicago: University of Chicago, 1981).
[24] *ThesCRA* II, 3.d (see p. 1, n. 2) "Heroisierung und Apotheose," p. 213.
[25] Ibid., 213–14.
[26] Brown, *The Cult of the Saints* (see above n. 23) 21.

heavy with the fullness of a beloved person."[27] And it was not just the popular, vulgar masses but also the Christian literate elite who could take comfort and strength from their physical, personal intimacy with the bodily remains of the saints who now, in union with their risen Lord, alive beyond death, could warmly intercede for them with God.

---

[27] Ibid., 139.

Part Five

Concluding Summary and Looking Ahead

It is hardly possible to overestimate the complexity of the topic of sacrifice in pagan and Christian Antiquity. The amount of data that needs to be selected and synthesized is overwhelming and continues to grow. The old assumptions that enabled scholars to write broad-brushed descriptions of sacrifice in antiquity are not just "in general" out of style in this postmodern age, these assumptions have also been found by much recent scholarship to be "in particular"—that is, in relation to this particular topic—embarrassingly procrustean retrojections into antiquity of flawed modern, often misunderstood, Christian ideas of sacrifice. Thus, much of what this book has tried to do is revisit and deconstruct. But, *quis custodiet custodes*? Who will guard the guards? Who will deconstruct our deconstruction?

The bias, the agenda, with which this book was originally approached was the desire to include in it, as an integral part of its historical data, the specifically trinitarian concept of Christian sacrifice that has been the fruit of my own decades-long research. That has to some extent been accomplished first, by our exposition (pp. 107–10), of the classical eucharistic anaphoras of Chrysostom and Basil, and second, by the inclusion immediately thereafter of the excursus "A trinitarian view of sacrifice." Yet the basic methodology that governs this whole book, however influenced it might be by an inevitable Christian theological bias, is not primarily theological; it remains within the trajectory of traditional historical criticism and Christian historical theology—the Christian "story," if you will—as that, over the past century, is being told and retold.

But modern hermeneutics, especially in its recent developments, compels us to attend carefully to the question: Who is telling the story? For it is the survivors, especially the surviving winners, who get to tell the story, who get to control how, by whom, and why the story is being told. These winners are, for the most part, Christians, and not just "Christianity" as such, or Christians in general, but the Christian elite. Almost everything in writing that has come to us from the ancient world has come to us in the "voice" of this or that Christian author and/or via the pens of countless Christian scribes, often Christian monks, copying out for posterity those works that happened to be in their possession and that they deemed worthy of preservation. If, for example, because of the scarcity of historical data, there are serious gaps in the story that the winning Christians tell even of their own early liturgical practices, how much deeper, wider, and more arbitrary must be the gaps in the stories that the Christians tell of pagan liturgical practices, or in the stories that the Christians deign to allow the pagans to tell of themselves? Gradually, modern research methods in a variety of disciplines, along with an increasingly cultivated hermeneutical suspicion of all traditionally transmitted stories, are enabling contemporary scholars to begin to piece together an at least somewhat more accurate picture of the practice of and attitudes toward sacrifice in Antiquity and Christianity.

This small book, the result of some five decades of theological and historical research into the concept of Christian sacrifice that has now been brought into conversation with a recent and much briefer foray into sacrifice in non-Christian Antiquity, has come up with a number of interesting findings, some of which I will briefly list here.

One striking finding is the degree of genuine similarity—at least among the literate elite—between Christian and non-Christian attitudes and practices regarding sacrifice in Antiquity. This goes beyond the simplistic anti-religious reductionism or apologetic *praeparatio evangelica* (preparation-for-the-gospel) interpretations that have often characterized the Christian accounts of such findings. We can now more readily recognize and honor constructively such things as the wisdom-literature similarities between the ethical exhortations of Hesiod's *Works and Days* and similar teachings in the Hebrew Scriptures. No longer compelled by a narrow exclusivism to assume that the Christian story is the only story that has merit, the Christian scholar can appreciate the remarkable temporal coincidence that the Hebrew tradition (and the Christian tradition in continuity with it) by way of the path of revelation was arriving at remarkably similar metaphorizing/spiritualizing concepts of sacrifice as was, by way of the path of reason, the Greek religious-philosophical tradition, and can appreciate further that, at the same time, an analogous development was taking place via Buddhism in the Far East.

This remarkable confluence of the "path of reason" and the "path of revelation" was manifest in a number of ways. One particularly striking convergence, now in the Roman imperial period, is in the "natural theology" of the Neoplatonists Plotinus, Porphyry, Iamblichus, and their followers. Their concept of a transcendent or spiritual Divinity that has no need of material sacrifice—and that sacrifice was therefore for human, not for divine, benefit—that concept of Divinity and of sacrifice is, at least philosophically speaking, barely distinguishable from the idea of God that was taking shape in the writings of the (basically also) Platonizing Christian ecclesiastical writers. Although Iamblichus's insistence, against his fellow Neoplatonist and probable mentor, Porphyry, on the need for material sacrifice made him, on the one hand, more "pagan," and the apparent theological inspiration for the re-paganizing programs of the emperor Julian, that insistence was, on the other hand, and religio-psychologically speaking, not very distant from the practical incarnationalism of the Christian teachers. Further, Iamblichus's insistence, that one needed to be already an initiate in the mysteries in order to be able to understand the sacrificial theurgy that he was expounding, is strikingly similar to the mystagogy that the Christian Fathers of the Church were preaching just a few decades later.

The similarities between the pagan and Christian literate elites are also striking. These people may well have had more in common with each other than with their own popular masses. An obvious example of this is the anti-sacrificial polemic of the Christian writers. The Christians did not have to invent this polemic. The substance, and often the very words, of the polemic they sought, they could find ready-made for them in the writings of their pagan contemporaries. Even the polemical strategy was similar. One did not normally polemicize against the thought and writings of the elite in the other camp, but against the popular, simplistic ideas and practices of the unenlightened masses in the other camp. Lucian, the "king" of the pagan satirists, is a striking example of this (see 2.8., pp. 36–38). His polemic against sacrifice and its attendant practices was not directed against the elevated ideas of divinity being taught by the philosophers and the more sophisticated among the teachers of the mysteries—he could presumably at least think of identifying with those—but against the traditional simplistically anthropomorphic ideas about, and the scandalous antics of, the gods of Greek mythology. There were, of course, some marvelous exceptions to this self-serving strategy, most notably, perhaps, in the sophisticated attack on Christians by the pagan Celsus in the late second century, and the equally sophisticated Christian response by Origen (see above, pp. 95–96) some seven decades later.

Another striking finding is the extent of the significance—often underestimated by Christian scholars—of the "luck of history": the fact that, from the time of Constantine, except for the brief reign of Julian the Apostate (361–63 CE), the emperors were Christian and aggressively favorable to the Christian cause. Christians happily see this as an act of divine providence assuring the eventual triumph of Christianity. One can only speculate how different history might have been had this not been the case. By the end of the fourth century, when the eventual triumph of Christianity seemed inevitable, and when the offering of state-sponsored public animal sacrifices had begun to be outlawed, most of the Roman senators and members of the elite ruling classes were apparently still pagan, not yet converted to Christianity, still resisting the increasing pro-Christian imperial pressure.[1] By then, half of the general population, especially in the cities, might well have been nominally Christian. But the long and not always forward-moving process of assimilation and Christianization of pagan customs and practices that was needed to make Christianity "popular" or humanly viable in its own right was still in its infancy. That Justinian, well into the sixth century, found it necessary to fulminate against "the error of the unholy and wicked pagans ... who offer sacrifices to insensate idols" (*Codex Justinianum* 1.11.10) gives some idea just how slow was the process by which Christianity eventually succeeded in becoming what might be called a "full-service religion."[2] How might history have been different had the post-Constantinian emperors not been Christian, or if the brilliant young pagan Julian (emperor 361–63) had enjoyed a long and successful reign? Would one still be able to claim, as this book has strongly claimed, that the Christians had a more compelling "story/discourse" about sacrifice?

In the end we are left with a number of significant further questions. Did, as we have been assuming, the Christian and pagan literate elites actually have

---

[1] See Cameron, *The Last Pagans of Rome* (see p. ix, n. 3) *passim*.
[2] See MacMullen, *Christianity and Paganism* (see p. 127, n. 13) 146.

more in common with each other than with their own illiterate masses? The provisional answers we can now give will depend a great deal on the nature and strength of the assumptions (bias) that we bring to the question. The committed Christian might tend to minimize the similarities and maximize the differences, and also might well challenge how great might be the differences between the Christian elite and the Christian masses. The committed historical critic (whether or not also religiously or secularly motivated) might well tend toward the opposite. The truth probably lies somewhere in between.

Related to this: just how valid is the idea of a "second church" as proposed by Ramsay MacMullen in 2009, and the implications of this for the cult of the martyrs and our understanding of early liturgical history.[3] Scholars probably need more time to chew on this.

As we conclude, we must stress how much this is a book written in a time of transition. The adequacy of the historical and hermeneutical presuppositions of several decades ago have been challenged, but not yet been replaced by other presuppositions with which most scholars can comfortably agree. For example, one helpful "model" for making sense of what was happening or presumably "going forward" in the various interactions between pagans and Christians—the "winner-loser" model—was comfortably presupposed by most of the scholarship that has gone into this book. But recently, the "gradual assimilation" model, as apparently favored in the recent magisterial works of both Alan Cameron and Peter Brown,[4] has been offering itself as not only, possibly, more helpful, but also, possibly, more faithful to the increased nuance that contemporary scholarship can bring to the study of Antiquity. This suggests that we should not assume that there eventually ever will be, or even should be, such a comfortable agreement—let alone any comfortably *excluding* agreement—on any such "model." We can only hope that what we have written may be moving in—and may be helping others to be moving in—what will turn out to be a helpful direction.

Fin.

---

[3] MacMullen, *The Second Church* (see above p. 9, n. 17).
[4] See p. ix, n. 3, and p. 2, n. 3.

Index of Names

The most important page numbers are printed in bold.

Abel   54, 59, 61
Abraham   59, 67, 72
Alexander   27, 28, 29
Ambrose   19, 40 n.52
Anaximenes   **27–9**, 131
Anebo   38, 40
Angenendt, Arnold   26 n.10, 27 n.13
Antiochus Epiphanes IV   67
Aphrahat   **99**
Apollonius   **33–4**, 38, 87, 132
Aristotle   27, 27 n.15, 29, 30, 35 n.39, 68, 100
Arnold, Russell C. D.   68 n.27
Artemis   21, 34
Athanasius   114
Athenagoras of Athens   **83**, 98
Attridge, Harold W.   79 n.49
Auffarth, Christoph   127 n.12
Augustine   19, 40 n.52, 95, **96–7**, **100–2**, 108, **120**, 131
Avery-Peck, Alan J.   68 n.28

Barnabas   **89**
Basil the Great   **98**, 111, 119, 135
Baumgarten, Joseph M.   68 n.22, 69 nn.29, 31, 33
Bernays, Jacob   29 n.16
Betz, Hans Dieter   35 n.42
Betz, Johannes   94 n.85, 95 n.88, 94 n.85, 95 n.88, 97 n.96, 98 nn.97, 100, 103, 99 nn.106, 107, 100 n.110
Blandina   87
Bradbury, Scott   39 n.48, 44 n.53
Bradshaw, Paul F.   72 n.36
Braulik, Georg   65 n.17
Brown, Peter   2, 2 n.3, 106–7, 122, 132 nn.23, 26, 139
Brox, Norbert   77 n.47
Bumazhnov, Dimitry   99 n.109
Burkert, Walter   14 n.27

Burns, J. Patout   18 n.39, 86 n.69
Burrus, Virginia   106 n.119

Caecilius   92
Caesarius of Arles   10
Cain   54, 59, 61
Cameron, Alan   ix, ix n.3, 2, 2 n.3, 7 nn.13, 14, 8, 10, 19–20, 105 n.17, 129 n.17, 138 n.1, 139
Cancik, Hubert   123 n.3, 127 n.12
Carter, Jeffrey   13 n.25
Casel, Dom Odo   99
Cavalieri, Pius Franchi de   80 n.52
Celsus   18, 18 n.39, 96 n.92, 138
Chilton, Bruce   68 n.28, 74 n.38
Chrysostom, John   40 n.52, 99, 99 n.108, 108, 111, 112, 119, 120, 135
Cicero   123
Clarke, Emma C.   39 n.50, 40 n.53, 46 n.57
Clarke, Graeme Wilber   93 n.79
Clement of Alexandria   87, **89–92**, 95–6, 102
Clement of Rome   **81**, **116**
Commodus   83 n.60
Constantine   19, 50, 109, 130, 138
Constantius   47
Cuming, G. J.   105 n.16
Cyprian   **94–5**, 119 n.38
Cyril of Alexandria   114
Cyril of Jerusalem   40 n.52, 45

Daly, Robert J.   viii, 5 nn.9, 10, 17 n.36, 18 n.39, 32 n.26, 59 n.12, 60 n.13, 63 n.16, 67 n.20, 68 n.21, 69 nn.29, 31, 32, 70 n.34, 72 n.36, 74 n.39, 75 n.43, 77 n.47, 80 n.53, 81 n.55, 82 n.58, 83 n.61, 85 n.64, 86 nn.67, 69, 87 n.70, 89 n.74, 95 n.90, 100 n.111, 102 n.112, 110 n.122, 113 n.127, 118 n.134

Index of Names

Daniélou, Jean   87 n.70
Daniel, Suzanne   75 n.40
David (King)   60, 67
Davies, John G.   108
Davies, William D.   68 n.28
Decius   11, 80 n.52, 103, 106
Democritus   37
Diéz/Rodriguez, Martinez   80 n.51
Dillon, John M.   39 n.50, 40 n.53, 46 n.57
Diocletian   11, 80 n.52, **124 n.6**
Dockter. *See under* Nesselrath, Theresa
Drake, Harold A.   127 n.13

Eckhardt, Benedikt   94 n.87
Eleazar   67
Empedocles   32
Ephrem   **97, 99**, 100 n.110
Esau   60
Eusebius   33, **97–8**, 124 n.7

Fahey, Michael A.   114 n.129
Falk, Daniel K.   68 n.28
Faraone, C. A.   6, n.12
Feldmaier, Reinhard   77 n.47
Felicitas   87
Ferguson, Everett   94 nn.83, 87, 97 nn.94, 95, 131 n.21
Finkelstein, Louis   68 n.28
Finlan, Stephen   85 n.66, 113, 128 n.16
Fortenbaugh, William W.   29 n.17
Fox, Robin Lane   34 n.33
Frank, Karl Suso   94 n.92
Füglister, Notker   65 n.17

Galerius   124 n.6
Gärtner, Bertil E.   69 n.33
Gibson, Mel   56
Girard, René   x, 4, 4 n.7, 14 n.27
Goodenough, Erwin Ramsdell   87 n.70
Goppelt, Leonhard   77 n.47
Gregory of Nazianzus   **98**
Gregory of Nyssa   **98**
Griffiths, John Gwyn   35, 35 n.41
Grisbrooke, W. Jardine   108
Gross, K.   80 n.53

Haarse   26 n.12
Hadas, Moses   35 n.36
Hahn, Ferdinand   77 n.47
Hammerton-Kelly, Robert G.   14 n.27

Harnack, Adolf von   95 n.91
Hecate   21, 23–4
Heim, Mark S.   5 n.10
Helgeland, John   18, n.39, 86 n.69
Heliodorus   **34–5**
Helios   50
Heraclides   96 n.92
Heraclitus   21, 26, 37
Hershbell, Jackson P.   39 n.50, 40 n.53
Hesiod   15, **21–6**, 30, 36, 54, 125, 130–1, 136
Heyman, George   6, 6 n.12, 11, 15, 17 n.37, 72 n.37, 129 n.18
Hickman, Hoyt L.   4 n.8
Hippolytus   **85, 118**, 119 n.136
Hobsbawm, Eric   31 n.22
Homer   15, 21, 36, 130 n.20
Horburg, William   68 n.28
Hosea   18
Houtman, Alberdina   6 n.11
Hubert, Henri   3, 4, 4 n.5, 5, 6

Iamblichus   7, 34 n.31, 38, **39–46**, 47–50, 101, 107, 113, 128, 129, **137**
Iapetus   22
Ignatius of Antioch   10, 17, **82**, 83, 103, 109, **117**
Irenaeus   **83–5, 118**
Irrazaval, Diego   17 n.36
Isaac   59, 90
Isaiah   18
Ixion   36

Jacob   60
Jakov, Daniel   121 n.1
James, King (Bible)   67 n.19
Janz, Denis R.   106 n.119
Jasper, R. C. D.   105, n.16
Jaspers, Karl   1
Jeremiah   18
Jerome   66
Jesus   61, 73
Johnson, Maxwell   11, 11 n.20, 106 n.119, 109
Julian the Apostate   34 n.33, 39, 44, 46, 46 n.60, 47, 50, 110, 130, 132, 137, 138
Justinian   138
Justin Martyr   **82–3**, 85, 89, **117–18, 118 n.133**

Käsemann, Ernst 76 n.46
Katz, Steven T. 69 n.28
Kharlamov, Vladimir 85 n.66, 113, 128 n.16
Kilmartin, Edward J. x, 3 n.4, 57 nn. 7, 8, **114 n.129**, 131 n.21
Klein, Hans 9 n.109
Klein, Richard 50 n.65
Kleist, James H. 104 n.115, 105
Klinzing, Georg 68 n.26
Knust, Jennifer Wright 6 n.12

Lactantius 80 n.52, **97**, 124
Lange, Armin 68 n.25
Leonard 94 n.87
Lieserung, E. 80 n.52
Lucian 8, 18, 35 n.39, **36–8**, 137
Luke 29, 55, 61, 108, 115

McClymond, Katherine 4 n.6, 6, 6 n.11, 12, 53
McGowan, Andrew B. 72 n.36
Macleod, Matthew D. 36 n.44
MacMullen, Ramsay 9, 9 n.17, 10, 105, 127 n.13, 138 n.2, 139
Macrobius 19, **51**, 106
Malachi 84, 93
Marcus Aurelius 83 n.60
Mark 29, 55, 61, 108, 115
Marx-Wolf, Heidi 8 n.15, 46
Matthew 61, 63, 71, 108, 115
Mauss, Marcel 3, 4, 4 n.5, 5, 6
Meijer, P. A. 31 n.25
Melito of Sardis 86
Menander 18
Metzinger, Adalbertus 65 n.17
Meyer, Hans Bernhard 114 n.129
Michel, Otto 76 n.46, 79 n.49
Mihoc, Vasile 99 n.109
Milavec, Aaron 80 n.53, 116 n.132
Minucius Felix **92–3**
Moses 14, 59, 65, 67, 90
Moss, Candida 103 n.114
Most, Glenn W. 21 n.3
Muhlenkamp, Christine 80 n.51

Naegle, August 99 n.108
Naiden, F. S. 6 n.12
Nesselrath, Theresa viii n.2, 68 n.21, 93 n.80, 87 n.93

Neusner, Jacob 68 n.28
Niehbuhr, Karl-W. 99 n.109
Noah 54, 59, 60, 127
Nock, Arthur Darby 46 n.58, 47
Noetus 118–19
Norden, Eduard 33 n.30

Obbink, Dirk 29 n.17, 30 n.18, 31 n.21, 32
Octavius (Minucius Felix) 92–3
Origen x, xi, 2, 8, 18, 18 n.39, 46, 53 n.3, 75 n.41, 86, 87, 88, **95–7**, **100–2**, 108, 114, 138

Paul (St.) 32, 45, 55, 70, 71, 72, 73, **74–5**, 76, 78, 82, 89, 99, 108, 115, 123
Peregrinus 37
Persepone 21
Perses 25
Peter (St.) 99
Petropoulou, Maria-Zoe 6, 6 n.12, 131 n.22
Pharaoh 14
Philo 18, **32–3**, 75, **87–9**, 90, 92
Philostratus the Elder 33, 34
Pilario, Daniel 17 n.36
Plato 15, 19, 26, 29, 31, 44, 68, 132
Pliny 80 n.52
Plotinus 38, 39, 132, 137
Plutarch 35
Polycarp 10, 17, **103–6**
Poorthuis, Marcel 6 n.11
Porphyry 7, 29, 30, 33, 35 n.39, **38–9**, 40, 42, 46, 102, 137
Pötscher, Walter 22, 23 n.6
Power, David N. 3 n.4, **119**
Praetextatus 19
Prometheus 22–3
Pythagoras 30, 38

Renaud, Bernard 95 n.87
Renz, Franz Ser. 94 n.83, 95 n.88
Rives, James B. 126 n.10
Rordorf, Willy 94 n.86
Rüpke, Jörg 123 n.3
Russell, Norman 85 n.66, 113, 128 n.16

Sallust 38, 39, **46–9**, 50
Samuel (prophet) 18
Sandt, Huub van de 81 n.53, 116 n.132

Sandy, Gerald N.   34 n.35
Saul (King)   60
Saxer, Victor   94 n.86
Scheid, John   126 n.11
Schlegel, Catherine M.   22 n.5
Schlier, Heinrich   76 n.46
Schmid, Herbert   94 n.87
Schuller, Eileen, M.   68 n.28
Schwartz, E.   119 n.136
Schwartz, Joshua   6 n.11
Seidensticker, Philipp   76 n.46
Seneca   26
Sharples, Robert W.   29 n.17
Sheerin, Daniel J.   119 n.137
Smith, Jonathan Z.   14 n.27
Socrates   26, 31, 90, 131
Solomon   72
Spicq, Ceslas   77 n.47, 79 n.49
Stephen (St.)   73
Stevenson, Kenneth W.   119 n.137
Stroumsa, Guy G.   6, 6 n.12, 58 n.11
Stuiber, Alfred   80 n.52
Sturdy, John   69 n.28
Susin, Luiz Carlos   17 n.36
Symmachus   15, 19, 41, **49–50**, 51, 101, 106, 110, 122

Tantalus   36
Tarkovsky, Andrei   57 n.6
Tertullian   16 n.32, 80 n.51, **93–4**
Theodore of Mopsuestia   40 n.52, 120
Theophrastus   **29–32**, 38, 43, 44, 128
Toulouse, Stéphane   102

Tov, Emanuel   68 n.25
Trier, Lars   57 n.6
Turner, Yossi   6 n.11

Ullucci, Daniel C.   xi, 2, 2 n.3, 6, 6 n.12, 9, 13, 14 n.26, 16 n.33, 17 n.35, 18, 19, 53, 56, 75, 129 n.18

Várhelyi, Zsuzsanna   6 n.12
Versnel, Hendrik S.   31 n.25
Vogt, J.   80 n.52
Völker, Walter   87 n.70
Voutiras, Emmanuel   121 n.1

Waldner, Katharina   123 n.3, 125
Watteville, Jean de   93 n.79, 94 nn.83, 87, 95 n.89, 97 n.94
Weigold, Matthias   68 n.25
Weinfield, Henry   22
West, Martin L.   25 n.7, 26
Wilckens, Ulrich   77 n.46
Wolfson, Harry Austryn   87 n.70

Xenophon   26

Yahweh   60
Young, Frances   98 nn.97, 99, 101, 102, 99 n.105
Young, Robin Darling   105–7

Zanella, Armin   68 nn.24, 25, 69 n.30
Zeus   22, 23, 25, 31, 36

Subject Index

The most important page numbers are printed in bold.

acceptance (divine) of sacrifice   16, 32, 55, **60–2**, 83, 88
access to divinity   46
acropolis   31
acts of the martyrs   103, 109
Adversus omnes Haereses (Irenaeus)   83–5, 118
Aethiopica   **34–5**
Africa   92
agriculture   31
Akedah (sacrifice of Isaac)   59
Alexandria, Alexandrian   32, 33, 46, **78–92**, 95
allegory, allegorical interpretation   32, 88, 89, 90
almsgiving   62, 87, 131
altar   33, 82, 86, 88, 89, 92, 96, 101
anabatic   44
anamnesis, anamnetic   30, 104, 108–9, 116, 128
anaphora   102, 104, 106, **107–10**, 112, 114; *see also* Eucharistic Prayer
anaphora of Basil   112
anaphora of Chrysostom   112
"Ancient Religion"   106
animal sacrifice   30–1, 35
anthropology   41, 46
anthropomorphism, anthropomorphic   25, 37, 40, 127, 137
antipathy (Christian-Jewish)   73
anti-sacrifice critique   **36–8**
apocalyptic   125
apocryphal   125
apologist(s), apologetic   **82–3**, 92, 93, 125
apostolic activity as sacrifice   79
apotropaic   64
apportionment of sacrifice   12, 23–4, 130
appropriation of sacrificial language   74
Aramaic   67
archaeology   9, 105
Arianism   18, 111

Aristotelian   101
assimilation   138–9
association of sacrifice   12
atheism   31, 35
Athens   29, 132
Athens and Jerusalem   116
atonement   55, 56, 62, **63–5**, 67, 83, 84, 98, 125, **127–8**
authority (over sacrifices)   28
axial age   1

Babylonian Exile   63, 64
baptism   130
baptism of blood   130
Barnabas, Epistle of   **89**
basilica(s)   109, 110, 114
bias   2, 11, 110, 135, 139
bishop(s)   7, 10, 105, 112, 127
blood, sacrificial   64
bloodless   83, 87; *see also* unbloody
blood of the covenant   115
blood rite   64, **65–7**, 115–16
body (ecclesial)   112
bones of the martyrs   104
bouphonia   31
Breaking the Waves (film)   57
breathing together   91–2
Buddhism   15, 137
burnt offering   59, 60, 90–1, 104; *see also* holocausts

calculation of the offering   23
cannibalism   31
Cappadocian Fathers   98–9, 114
catechism   47
categories (of people)   19, 20
Catholic(s), Roman   3, 4, 5, 56–7, 64
Catholic sacrifice   **56–7**
cemeteries   10, 114, 132
Christ, sacrifice of   17, 75
Christ (both priest and victim)   95

Christianization   138
Christian Sacrifice   xi, 2, 57–8
Christic   70
Christ mysticism   103
Christologize   55
Christology, Christological   81, 86, 120
Church, oblation of the   84, 92
Church Fathers; *see* Fathers of the Church
City of God (Augustine)   120
Clement of Rome, Epistle of   **81**, 116–17
Colloquium on Violence and Religion (COV&R)   x
Colosseum   82
communion sacrifice   115
communion with divinity   45, 128
Community Rule (Qumran)   69
Concerning the Gods and the Universe   **46–9**
confession(al) (beliefs)   5
confession (of sins)   81
Confucianism   15
Constantinian   10
consumption of sacrifice   12, 23, 130
contemplation   89
control (church's)   10
conversion   19, 130
Corinthian(s)   75
cosmos   15, 129
cost of sacrifices   28–9
Counter-Reformation   119
covenant sacrifice   71
criticism, historical   ix
critique(s) of sacrifice   16, 18, 125
crucifixion   3, 4, 75, 94
cult criticism   83, 90
cult of the martyrs   19, 110, 132, 139
cultural development   32
culture(s)   ix, 1, 6, 8, 14, 18, 19, 21, 31, 74
custom   21–2

daemon (personal)   42
De Abstinentia (Porphyry)   29–30, 38
Dead Sea Scrolls   **68–9**; *see also* Qumran
deception   22–3
Decius, persecution of   103
deconstruction   x, 2, 12
De divinatione (Cicero)   123
definition of sacrifice   xi, 8, 13, 18, 28, 53, 100, 111, 120; *see also* meanings

degeneration (religious)   32
deification, divinization, theosis   85, 98, 103, 128, 132
Delphi   34, 35
De Mysteriis (Iamblichus)   **38–46**, 48
De Sacrificiis (Lucian)   **36–8**
destruction of sacrificial victim   28, 54, 110
development   31
diachronic structure of this book   121
Dialogue with Trypho (Justin)   117
Diaspora   16, 62, 125
diatribe   36
Didache   **80–1**, 116
Didyma (Apollo)   124
diptychs   108–9
discourse   129
discourse(s), sacrificial   15, 49, 107, 138
discursive, pre-discursive   114
dispositions for sacrifice   31, 32, 54, 55, 61, 62, 64, 77, 88, 131
divination   40, 42, **123–5**
Divine Liturgy   99
divine presence   43
divine providence   138
divinity, concept of   137
divinization; *see* deification
division, distribution of sacrifice   22
domestic animals   30
Donatism, Donatists   27, 91
dramatists   18

Early Christianity   79
East, the   96, 100
East Syrian   119
eating the sacrifice   11
ecclesiology, ecclesiological   82, 120
economics of sacrifice   54, **130–1**
ecumenic(al)   4
ecumenical councils   111
effect(s) of sacrifices   47, 48
efficacy of sacrifice(s), cause of the   44
Egyptian authority   15
Egyptian religion   14
elite(s)   2, **7–8**, 14, 16, 17, 24, 34, 37, 38, 61, 68, 82, 88, 106, 107, 110, 111, 114, 122, 124, 127–9, 131, 133, **136**, 137, 138
embolism   108–9, 112
emperor cult   126

Subject Index

emperor(s)   7, 10, 11, 37, 46, 50, 80, 97, 106, 110, 124, 126, 130, 132, 137, 138
empire   15
end of paganism?   **19–20, 50**
epiclesis, epicletic   30, 104, 108–9, 112, 128
Epicurean   18
epistles (New Testament)   **74–9**
Epistle to the Romans (Ignatius)   117
eschatology   120
ethical sacrifice   **78**
ethics, ethical   16, 24, 70, 89, 125
ethics and sacrifice   **125–7**
Ethiopic Tales   **34–5**
etiology   23, 30, 104
Eucharist, eucharistic   3, 56, 71, 81, 82, 83, 84, 86, 92, 94, 97, 98, 99, 102–3, 106, 130
Eucharist and atonement   98
Eucharist as sacrifice   **114–20**
The Eucharistic Mystery (Power)   **119–20**
Eucharistic Prayer(s)   71, 81, 111, 113, 116, 128, 131, 135; see also anaphora
eucharistizing   81
euergetism   131
example of Christ and martyrs   107
exchange   11
Exile   16, 62, 125
Exodus   14, 65
expiation   66

faith document   45
fasting   62
Fathers of the Church   8, 56, 111, 128, 137
fifth century   51, 107–8, 111, 115
first century   115–16
first fruits   31, 43, 48, 84
flood, the   59
fourth century   16, 18, 33, 50, 51, 66, 107, 109, 110, 111, 113, 138
functionalist theory of sacrifice   30

general sacrifice   54, 55
gnosis, gnostic, Gnosticism   19, 56, 79, 83, 84, 85, **89–91**, 96
God, One High   107
golden age (patristic)   71, 88, 119
good works   62

gospel as priestly service   76
gospels   **73–4**
great story   5
Greco-Roman   **21–51**
  religion(s)   46, 49, 58
  sacrifice   14
  traditions   32
  world   15
Greek
  culture   67
  dramatists   18
  East   100
  influence   17
  philosophy, philosophers   26, 77, 88, 127
  religious philosophy   47
  satirists   18
  tradition   136
  West   100
guardian angels   42
gymnosophists   35

haggadah   86
hagiography   34, 87
hands, laying on of   64
healing   62
heart (human) as altar   101
heating of sacrifice   12
heaven   49, 101
heavenly liturgy   69
Hebrew
  faith   88
  prophets   31, 127
  sacrifice (biblical)   54
  Scriptures   16, 18, 24, **58–67**, 91, 136
Hebrews, Epistle to the   78, **79**
hecatomb   34
hermeneutic(s), hermeneutical   ix, **1–20**, 53, 135, 136, 139
heroes, saints as   11, 104, 114
heroes and saints   **132–3**
highest god   38
high priest   32, 33, 79, 88, 90–1, 97, 104
Hinduism   15
historical critic   139
historical data, paucity of   108
historical Jesus   72
historical structure of this book   121
historiography   37
history, historical   2, 136

history, sacrifice in **13–17**
history of religions   ix, **3–5**, 6, 53, 56, 110
holocaust(s)   90–1, 104; *see also* burnt offering
Holy Spirit   57, 77, 98, 104–5, 111, 112
How to Write History (Lucian)   37
human sacrifice   31, 35
hunter-gatherers   13

identification of sacrifice   12
idolatry, 17, 82
idols   138
imitation of Christ   87, 94, 95
imitation of divinity/the gods   49, 107
Incarnation, incarnational   45, 70, 83, 85, 89, 90, 94, 96, 101–2, 118, 137
institutionalizing   81
Institution Narrative; *see* Words of Institution
institution of the Eucharist   **115**; *see also* Words of Institution
intelligentsia   37, 90
internet   2
interpretation of sacrifice   9, 13, 32, 88
intertestamental Judaism   67
invented tradition/history   31
Isaac-Christ typology   90
Islam   80, 123

Jainism   15
Jerusalem, Athens and   16
Jewish
    culture   6
    prophets   29
    Study Bible   60, 66
    traditions   14, 32
Judaism   9, 15, 80, 123
Judean   18

katabatic   44
killing of the sacrifice   11, 12

Lamb of God   90
Last Supper   71, 99, 103
Late Biblical Judaism   16
Latin Theology   93
Latin West   100
Law (Torah)   17, 55, 62, 72
Lent   55
Letter to Anebo (Porphyry)   40

Letter to the Churches of Vienne and Lyons   87
Leviticus, Book of   59
Leviticus 17:11   66
lex talionis   66
Life of Apollonius   **33–4**
linear development   108
liturgical-historical data   71
liturgy, liturgical   x, 5
living sacrifice(s)   77
living stones   77–8, 96
logikē thusia   47, 70, 98
Logos   88, 97

Maccabees, Maccabean   67, 103
made with hands   73, 78
Malachi, prophecy of   81, 116
martyrdom   10, 67, 82, 83, 86, 87, 91, 103, 106, 109
Martyrdom of Polycarp   **103–6**, 109
martyr(s)   10, 17, 99, 103, 104, 107, 130
martyrs, cult of   10, 11, **102–7**, 132
Mass, Sacrifice of the   3, 4, 56
masses (of people)   8, 110, 137, 139
material sacrifice   82, 93
Matthew 5:24   **62–3**, 73
meanings, of sacrifice   **53–8**; *see also* definition of sacrifice
meat(s), sacrificial   131
memorial   4
mercy, works of   17
metaphorical   11, 60
metaphoricize, metaphoricization   9, 113
method(s), methodologies   ix, **1–20**, 135, 136
Middle Platonism   35
mimetic theory   x
minority   19, 106
moment   65, 71, 111, 113
monetary value of sacrifices   26
monk(s)   2, 36, 136
monotheism   12
Moralia (Plutarch)   35
morality   125
Mystagogical Catecheses   40, 45
mystagogy   129, 137
mystery (Christian)   5, 97, 113
mystery, mysteries   45, 137
mystery cults/religions   50, 130
mystical   107

mysticism   87, 103
mythology   138
myth(s)   3, 13, 24, 25, 40, 107

Narrative of Institution   108–9; see also Words of Institution
natural theology   88, 137
Nazirite sacrifice, vow   72, 78
Neoplatonic, Neoplatonist(s)   45, 47, 113, 126, 128–9, 132, 137
Neoplatonism   8, 33, 38, 88, 101, 102
neo-Pythagorean   38
nephesh   66
New
    covenant   79, 84, 118
    oblation   84, 118
    Revised Standard Version (NRSV)   66
    Temple   57, 69, 79
    Testament   57, 67, **70–9**
Nicea, Council of   97, 109
Noah's sacrifice   60, 127
North Africa   27, 68, 100

objectivity   3, 5
Octavius (Minucius Felix)   92–3
offertory procession   131
Old Testament   67
Olympus, Olympian   8, 36, 49
On Piety (Theophrastus)   29
On Rhetoric (Aristotle)   27
On the Death of Peregrinus (Lucian)   37
orders (ranks) of the gods   106–7
origin of sacrifice   22
origins of religion, culture   14

paganism, decline of   46
paradigm change   19
participation (with divinity)   43
paschal lamb (Christ)   71
Passion of Christ   86, 95
Passion of SS. Perpetua and Felicitas   87
The Passion of the Christ (film)   57
Passover   32, 83, 86, 88, 90, 115, 116
    of Christ   95
    of the Christian   95
    in Egypt   65, 95
    Lamb (Christ)   115
    treatises   **86**
Patripassianism   118
Pauline communities   115

pax Christi   129
pax deorum   63, 122, 128, 129
Pelagianism   87
pentalogue   25
Pentateuch   59
Peri Pascha (Origen)   86, 95
Peripatos   29
persecution(s)   11, 80, 95, 103, 106, 109, 114, 124
perspective (bias), Christian   53
1 Peter 2:4–10   **77–8**
Philonic   101
philosopher(s)   8, 15, 16, 18, 33, 61, 107, 126, 137
philosophy, philosophical   15, 61, 82, 90
physical realism   84
piety towards the gods   30
Plato, cult of   132
Plato, Platonic, Platonism, Platonists   18, 40, 42, 44, 101, 102
Platonic dichotomy   43
Platonizing   137
poets   8
polemic(s), polemical   5, 8, 10, 34, 37, 82, 90, 93, 107, 137
politically correct   6
polytheism   12
polythetic, sacrifice as   11, 53
post-Constantinian   138
postmodern   **5–7**, 54
post-Nicene   100
praeparatio evangelica   136
prayer   21, 22, 23, 30, 36, 40, 43, 45, 46, 47, 48, 55, 61, 62, **68–9**, 92, 94, 96, 97, 99, 112, 115, **121–3**, 128
praying, eucharistic   109, 111
pre-Christological   116
pre-gospel   81
pre-history   13
pre-Nicene   100
presuppositions   139
priest   4, 112
procession (pagan sacrificial)   131
procrustean retrojections   135
profane, the   18
property   24
prophecy   104
prophets   16, 125
propitiation   21, 25, 84, 119
propitious   26

proselytizing 87
prosperity gospel 25
Protestant(s) 3, 4, 5, 56, 57, 64, 94
Psalms 118
pure sacrifice 84, 87
purpose of sacrifice 32, 42, 43, 44, 45, 48, **49**, 50, 83–4, 85, 88, 101, **127–9**
Pythagorean 33

Quartodeciman 86
quis custodiet custodes? 135
Qumran 62, **68–9**, 70, 75, 81

reach nichoach 60
Reallexikon für Antike und Christentum (RAC) x
reason, path of 16, 61, 136–7
reasonable sacrifice 25
reconciliation 62
reductionism 136
reform (pagan) of Julian 46
Reformation, Protestant 56, 64, 119
reinterpretation of sacrifice 17, 81
rejection
    of animal sacrifice 38
    of material sacrifice 131
    of sacrifice in general 9, 18, 126, 131
religio 122
religio licita 106
religious, the 18
religious authorities 126
re-paganizing 137
research 136
resistance (pagan) to Christianity 50
res publica 50
revelation, path of 16, 61, 129, 136–7
revisionism 32
rhetoric 9, 11, 57
rhetoric, sacrificial, of sacrifice 10, 17, 50, 72, 109, **129–30**
Rhetoric to Alexander (Anaximenes) **27–9**
ritual
    cultic, sacrificial 32, 46, 62, 115, 126, 129, 130
    of sin offering 64–5
    worship 42
Roman 18, 19
    religion 17, 18, 50, 122
    satirists 18
    senators 138

Romans, Epistle to the (Ignatius) 103
Romans, the 15
Rome 132
rubrics of sacrifice 44

Sacramentum Caritatis (Pope Benedict XVI) 56
The Sacrifice (film) 57
Sacrifice Unveiled (Daly) x, 57
sacrificium Christianorum (Augustine) 131
saints; *see* heroes
salvation history 72
1 Samuel 18
sancta societas (Augustine) 101, 120
sanctuaries (pagan) 124
sanctuary 33, 88
satire, satirists 8, 18, 36, 137
Saturnalia (Macrobius) 19, 51
scholarship, historical liturgical 110
scholarship, scholars ix, 1, 2, 3, 6, 7, 9, 15, 17, 59, 109, 114, 135, 138, 139
science, modern 4
second church (Ramsay) 10, 105, 139
secular sacrifice 54
selection of sacrifice 12
self-offering, sacrifice as 76
senatorial class 110
Septuagint (LXX) 61, 66, 67, 87
Sermon on the Mount 62
Servant Christology 116
Servant of God 90
Servant Songs 67
sin offering 13, **63–5**, 75, 83
Skeptic 18
Skirophorion 31
slaughtering of sacrificial victim 64
Smyrna 103
soul 90
soul as altar 33, 75, 89, 92, 94
spiritualize, spiritualization 9, 11, 16, 32, 55, 62, 69, **70**, 79, 80, 81, 88, 89, 92, 98, 102, 113, 115, 117, 125, 131
spiritual sacrifice(s) 15, **76**, 77, 87, 93
spiritual worship 45
Stoic, Stoicism 18, 26, 87, 126
story 11, 19, 127, **135–6**, 138
Structure of Eucharistic Prayers 108–9
structure of this book 121
struggle, pagan *vs.* Christian 18

studies, religious 4
substitution 12, 17, 64, **65–7**, 125
subversive 129
superstition 35
supreme god 34
survivors, winners 135
synchronic structure of this book 121
Syriac Church Fathers 99
systematic logic 41
systematic structure of this book 121

teaching 62
Temple, the 9, 16, 17, 62, 63, 68, 69, 72, 73, 74, 75, 78, 81, 88
   destruction of 78, 122, 125
   Second 63
temple(s) 33, 49, 92, 95–6, 101, 115–16
   body as 96
   community as 77
   theology 89
test, sacrifice as 80
Theogony (Hesiod) **21–5**
theology, theologian(s) x, 2, 19, 29, 30, 46, 53, 56, 57, 60, 61, 71, 82, 96, 98, 129, 135, 136
theology of sacrifice 38, **39–46**, 75, 76, 77, 79, 88, 126
theorizing (theological) 14
theory of sacrifice **39–46**, 106
theosis; *see* deification
Thesaurus Cultus et Rituum Antiquorum (*ThesCRA*) 1
theurgic ritual 41
theurgy 38, 40, 42, 43, 44, 107, 113–14, 129
theurgy, goal of 113–14
tombs; *see* cemeteries
Torah 16
tradition, pagan 50

transition 7
translation, translator 85
Trent, Council of 4
trial of Jesus 73
Trinity, trinitarian x, 56, 57, **110–14**, 135
true sacrifice 88

unbelief 47
unbloody sacrifices 92, 98; *see also* bloodless
union with divinity 107
universal priesthood 32, 88, **91**

vaticinium ex eventu 124, 125
Vedic culture 6
vegetal offerings 26
vegetarianism 30
Vergegenwärtigung 99
veritas Hebraica 66
vicarious atonement 67
victim 4, 56, 93
victim, destruction of 4, 5

War Scroll (Qumran) 69
welfare of the state as purpose of sacrifice 110
West, the 94, 96, 100, 120
widow's mite offering 29, 55
wisdom literature 136
wonder-worker 33
Words of Institution (Eucharist) 108–9, 112, 113, **115**
Works and Days (Hesiod) **21–6**, 125, 131, 136
world of sacrifice 11–13, 15, **17–19**

Yom Kippur 65

Zoroastrianism 15

www.ingramcontent.com/pod-product-compliance
Lightning Source LLC
Chambersburg PA
CBHW052050300426
44117CB00012B/2057